USING

filemaker®

bento

Jesse Feiler

800 East 96th Street, Indianapolis, Indiana 46240 USA

Using FileMaker® Bento

Copyright © 2010 by Pearson Education, Inc.

ISBN-13: 978-0-7897-4448-7

ISBN-10: 0-7897-4448-1

The Library of Congress Cataloging-in-Publication Data is on file.

Printed in the United States of America

First Printing: May 2010

Trademarks

Warning and Disclaimer

Bulk Sales

Que Publishing offers excellent discounts on this book when ordered in quantity for bulk purchases or special sales. For more information, please contact

U.S. Corporate and Government Sales

1-800-382-3419

corpsales@pearsontechgroup.com

For sales outside of the U.S., please contact

International Sales

international@pearson.com

Associate Publisher
Greg Wiegand

Acquisitions Editor
Loretta Yates

Development Editor
Todd Brakke

Managing Editor
Kristy Hart

Project Editor
Andy Beaster

Copy Editor
Language Logistics

Indexer
Lisa Stumpf

Proofreader
Jennifer Gallant

Technical Editor
Ryan Griggs

Publishing Coordinator
Cindy Teeters

Designer
Anne Jones

Compositors
Jake McFarland
Nonie Ratcliff

Contents at a Glance

Introduction

1   Bento: The Database for the Rest of Us

2   Using the Bento Window

3   Working with Bento Forms

4   Building a Bento Library from Your Own Data

5   Working with Phone, URL, IM, and Address Fields and Lists in Contacts

6   Working with Bento Fields and Calculations

7   Expanding the Inventory Library with Related Data Fields and Collections

8   Synchronizing with the Bento iPhone and iPad Apps

9   Sharing Data with Other Bento Users

10 Using Built-in Bento Libraries for Address Book and iPhoto

11 Using Built-in Bento Libraries for iCal Tasks and iCal Events

12 Working with Bento's Projects Library to Use Related Records from iCal Tasks, iCal Events, Apple Mail, and Address Book

13 Designing a Projects Library to Share on Your LAN and Synchronize with Your iPhone

14 Importing and Exporting Bento Data and Libraries

15 Using the Bento Template Exchange

Index

Media Table of Contents

To register this product and gain access to the Free Web Edition and the audio and video files, go to **quepublishing.com/using**.

Chapter 1:   **Bento: The Database for the Rest of Us**
Show Me **Media 1.1**—A video about using the Bento Window 10
Show Me **Media 1.2**—A video about setting Bento preferences 16

Chapter 2:   **Using the Bento Window**
Show Me **Media 2.1**—A video about creating a Notes library 29
Show Me **Media 2.2**—A video about using the Navigation Bar 30
Show Me **Media 2.3**—A video about creating a new record 34
Show Me **Media 2.4**—A video about printing records in Bento 38
Tell Me More **Media 2.5**—A discussion about the issues with
pasting data into table views 43

Chapter 3:   **Working with Bento Forms**
Show Me **Media 3.1**—A video about how to duplicate and
rename a form 52
Tell Me More **Media 3.2**—A discussion about how, when,
and why to use form tools... 53
Show Me **Media 3.3**—A video about applying a new
theme to a form 55
Show Me **Media 3.4**—A video about copying a form
within a library 61

Chapter 4:   **Building a Bento Library from Your Own Data**
Show Me **Media 4.1**—A video about using file references in Bento 67
Tell Me More **Media 4.2**—A discussion about checking your
data conversion 69
Show Me **Media 4.3**—A video about importing data into a
new Bento library 73
Show Me **Media 4.4**—A video about cleaning up a
spreadsheet to import 75

Chapter 5:   **Working with Phone, URL, IM, and Address Fields
and Lists in Contacts**
Show Me **Media 5.1**—A video about entering contact data 82
Show Me **Media 5.2**—A video about using a field and a list 85
Show Me **Media 5.3**—A video about editing contact data 86
Tell Me More **Media 5.4**—A discussion about time-shifting
your work by using Bento Buttons 86

Chapter 6:   **Working with Bento Fields and Calculations**
Show Me **Media 6.1**—A video about deleting, duplicating,
and renaming a field 92
Show Me **Media 6.2**—A video about creating a date/time field 96

Show Me **Media 6.3**—A video about creating a calculation 100
Tell Me More **Media 6.4**—A discussion about changing field types ... 105

Chapter 7:   **Expanding the Inventory Library with Related Data Fields and Collections**

Show Me **Media 7.1**—A video about creating an Ins & Outs library ... 110
Show Me **Media 7.2**—A video about creating a relationship
by dragging a library onto a form 112
Show Me **Media 7.3**—A video about adding a related data field 115
Show Me **Media 7.4**—A video about adding data to a related field ... 117
Show Me **Media 7.5**—A video about adding a related
data field and its data 117

Chapter 9:   **Sharing Data with Other Bento Users**

Show Me **Media 9.1**—A video about setting up Bento sharing 147
Show Me **Media 9.2**—A video about connecting to shared
libraries and databases 149
Tell Me More **Media 9.3**—A discussion about implementing
the best security 150
Show Me **Media 9.4**—A video about working with locked fields 154

Chapter 10:   **Using Built-In Bento Libraries for Address Book and iPhoto**

Tell Me More **Media 10.1**—A discussion about working
with Address Book Groups and Smart Collections 158
Show Me **Media 10.2**—A video about setting up iPhone
synchronization with iTunes 165
Show Me **Media 10.3**—A video about using data detectors 168
Show Me **Media 10.4**—A video about using the iPhoto library 170

Chapter 11:   **Using Built-In Bento Libraries for iCal Tasks and iCal Events**

Show Me **Media 11.1**—A video about searching iCal 173
Tell Me More **Media 11.2**—A discussion about the iCal
data structure. 176
Show Me **Media 11.3**—A video about using Mail's data
detectors with iCal 179
Show Me **Media 11.4**—A video about synchronizing iCal events 182

Chapter 12:   **Working with Bento's Projects Library to Use Related Records from iCal Tasks, iCal Events, Apple Mail, and Address Book**

Tell Me More **Media 12.1**—A discussion about getting the
most out of data integration 183
Show Me **Media 12.2**—A video about creating a good
Bento form design 184
Show Me **Media 12.3**—A video about adding an image to
your form with an image box 187
Show Me **Media 12.4**—A video about adding related records 191

Chapter 13:   **Designing a Projects Library to Share on Your LAN and Synchronize with Your iPhone**

Tell Me More **Media 13.1**—A discussion about related records 198
Show Me **Media 13.2**—A video about creating a related notes table 207
Show Me **Media 13.3**—A video about going to and from related records 210
Show Me **Media 13.4**—A video about enhancing the relationship 210

Chapter 14:   **Importing and Exporting Bento Data and Libraries**

Show Me **Media 14.1**—A video about creating a new table for imported data 217
Show Me **Media 14.2**—A video about importing data by pasting into table view 218
Show Me **Media 14.3**—A video about exporting Bento data 219
Tell Me More **Media 14.4**—A discussion about design considerations for templates 221

Chapter 15:   **Using the Bento Template Exchange**

Show Me **Media 15.1**—A video about exploring the Bento Template Exchange 225

Table of Contents

      Introduction **1**

1   **Bento: The Database for the Rest of Us** **7**

      Introducing Bento 7

          Looking at Bento 7

          It's All About Your Data 10

          Bento's Three Roles 11

          Bento Lets You Leap Over Boundaries 12

          How Much Programming Does Bento Require? 12

          What Does "Personal" Mean? 13

      Getting Started with Bento 14

      Understanding Bento Terminology 16

          Fields 17

          Records 21

          Libraries 22

          Collections 22

2   **Using the Bento Window** **25**

      Getting Around the Bento Window 25

          Create a Library 28

      Using the Records Area 29

          Introducing Table Views 30

          Introducing Grid Views 30

          Using Split Views 31

          Creating a New Record 33

          Entering Text Data 35

          Printing a Record 36

          Finding Data 38

          Using Advanced Find 39

          Deleting a Record 42

      Using Table Views in Bento 42

          Sorting a Table View in Bento 42

          Pasting Data into Table View in Bento (Part 1) 43

          Editing Fields with Table View in Bento 44

          Pasting Data into Table View in Bento (Part 2) 44

      Using the Libraries & Fields Pane 44

          Using Library Folders 45

          Using Library Icons 46

      Setting Bento Preferences 47

3 Working with Bento Forms **49**

Working with Forms 49

    Duplicate and Rename a Form 52

Customizing a Form with Themes 53

    Choose a Theme 54

Customizing a Form's Fields 56

    Copy Forms within a Library 60

4 Building a Bento Library from Your Own Data **63**

Getting Started Organizing Your Data 63

    Reviewing Your Legacy Data 64

    Working with Data Formats 64

Performing a Basic Data Import 67

    Import Data Into a New Bento Library 69

Cleaning Up Imported Data 74

5 Working with Phone, URL, IM, and Address Fields
and Lists in Contacts **77**

Exploring the Contacts Library 77

Working with Fields 81

    Enter Contact Data 81

Working with Address, Email, Phone Number, and URL Lists 82

Adding Address Fields and Lists to Your Forms 84

    Use a Field and a List 84

    Use Contact Data 85

6 Working with Bento Fields and Calculations **87**

Adding Calculation Fields to the Exercise Log 87

Creating and Formatting Date Fields in Exercise Log 89

    Creating a Stop Date Field 89

    Creating a Start Date Field 91

    Using Date and Time Field Controls 92

Creating and Formatting a Number Field in Exercise Log 95

Creating and Formatting Calculations in Exercise Log 96

    Working with the Calculation Dialog 96

    Creating the Duration Field 98

    Creating the Calories Burned Field 100

Creating and Formatting Choice Fields 101

Creating and Formatting Checkbox Fields 102

Creating and Formatting Currency Fields 103

Creating and Formatting Automatic Counter Fields 103

Creating and Formatting Rating Fields 104

Editing Bento Fields 104

**7 Expanding the Inventory Library with Related
Data Fields and Collections** **107**

Exploring the Inventory Library 107

Creating an Ins & Outs Library from Scratch 109

    Creating an Ins & Outs Library 110

Using Relationships to Track Inventory 112

    Creating a Relationship by Dragging a Library onto a Form 112

    Creating a Relationship by Adding a Related Data Field 114

    Formatting the Related Data Field 115

    Summarizing a Related Data Field 118

    Reviewing the Related Records 118

    Improving the Relationship and the Form 119

Using Collections 122

    Creating an Empty Collection 123

    Adding a Record to a Collection 123

    Creating a Collection from Selected Records 124

Using Smart Collections 125

**8 Synchronizing with the Bento iPhone
and iPad Apps** **129**

Sharing Versus Synchronization 129

Using the Bento iPhone or iPad App by Itself 131

Using the Bento iPad App 131

    Using the Bento App Home 133

    Searching the Libraries 134

    Creating a New Library 136

Working with a Bento iPhone App Library 137

Synchronizing Libraries Between your iPhone or iPad
    and your Computer 138

    Understanding "Same Wi-Fi Network" 138

    Doing Your First Sync 140

    Performing a Sync 144

Securing Your Bento Data on Your Mobile Device 144

9   Sharing Data with Other Bento Users **145**

Setting Up Sharing 145
  Set Up Bento Sharing 146

Using Shared Libraries and Databases 147
  Connect to Shared Libraries and Databases 148

Securing Your Data 149
  Use Encrypted Fields 150
  Use a Database Password 151
  Work with Locked Fields 152
  Using a Sharing Password 154

10   Using Built-In Bento Libraries for Address Book and iPhoto **155**

Exploring the Address Book Library 155

Extending Bento's Address Book Library with New
  Fields and Forms 158

Synchronizing Address Book 160
  Synchronizing Address Book with MobileMe 161
  Synchronizing Address Book with iPhone 164
  Synchronizing Address Book with PDAs and Other Devices 167
  Using MobileMe Push Technology to Synchronize Data 167

Using Mac OS X Data Detectors to Update Address Book 168

Exploring the iPhoto Library 169
  Use the iPhoto Library 170

11   Using Built-In Bento Libraries for iCal Tasks and iCal Events **171**

Catching Up with iCal 171
  Search iCal 172

Exploring the Bento iCal Libraries 176

Using Mail's Data Detectors with iCal 178
  Use Mail's Data Detectors with iCal 178

Managing Your Calendar Data 180

Synchronizing iCal Events 182

12   Working with Bento's Projects Library to Use Related Records from iCal Tasks, iCal Events, Apple Mail, and Address Book **183**

Exploring Projects 183
  Add an Image to Your Form with a Image Box 185

Working with Related Records from iCal and Address Book 187
    Adding Related Records 187

Working with Related Records from Mail 191

Customizing Fields and Revising Forms 192

Creating and Sharing Calendar Events and Address
    Book Contacts with MobileMe 193

**13   Designing a Projects Library to Share on Your LAN
        and Synchronize with Your iPhone** **195**

Taking Another Approach to Projects 195

Exploring the Projects Library 198

Organizing and Implementing Notes: The Basics 199
    Create a New Bento Library for Notes 200
    Create the Basic Field in Project Notes 202
    Add Related Data Fields to the Projects Library 203

Enhancing the Relationship 207

14   Importing and Exporting Bento Data and Libraries **213**

Importing and Exporting Basics 213
    Importing Data into an Existing Bento Library 213
    Exporting Bento Data 218

Importing and Exporting Libraries 220
    Exporting Bento Libraries as Templates 220
    Importing Bento Libraries as Templates 220

15   Using the Bento Template Exchange **223**

Exploring the Bento Template Exchange 223

Learning from the Bento Template Exchange 226

Sharing Your Templates 227

Index **231**

About the Author

Jesse Feiler has been designing databases and user-oriented solutions for two decades. He is the author of a number of books on Mac OS X, FileMaker, the Web, and a variety of other technologies such as Drupal, mashups, and Facebook. His most recent books are *Filemaker Pro 10 in Depth*, *Sams Teach Yourself Drupal in 24 Hours*, and *iWork '09 for Dummies*.

A member of the FileMaker Business Alliance, he is also a developer of solutions for small businesses, nonprofit organizations (particularly those in the arts fields), publishing, and production companies. He has done many FileMaker rehabs, bringing them up to modern standards and designs. His knowledge of FileMaker and Mac OS X technologies has helped him integrate tools such as Automator into FileMaker solutions—and now into Bento.

He has worked as a developer and manager for companies such as the Federal Reserve Bank of New York (monetary policy and bank supervision), Prodigy (early Web browser), Apple (information systems), New York State Department of Health (rabies and lead poisoning), The Johnson Company (office management), and Young & Rubicam (media planning and new product development).

Active in the community, he has served on a variety of nonprofit boards including those of HB Studio and Mid-Hudson Library System, as well as zoning and planning boards. He has conducted trustee training sessions for Clinton-Essex-Franklin Library System and other groups.

Feiler's website is northcountryconsulting.com.

Acknowledgments

Many people have contributed to this book, not least the wonderful people at FileMaker who have developed Bento. In particular, Kevin Mallon and Delfina Daves have, as always, provided wonderful assistance to the project. At Que Publishing, Loretta Yates, senior acquisitions editor, has helped to shape the book through the editorial process. It's been a pleasure to work with you.

At Waterside Productions, where Carole McClendon has, again, provided the support and assistance so important to an author.

We Want to Hear from You!

As the reader of this book, *you* are our most important critic and commentator. We value your opinion and want to know what we're doing right, what we could do better, what areas you'd like to see us publish in, and any other words of wisdom you're willing to pass our way.

As an associate publisher for Que Publishing, I welcome your comments. You can email or write me directly to let me know what you did or didn't like about this book—as well as what we can do to make our books better.

Please note that I cannot help you with technical problems related to the topic of this book. We do have a User Services group, however, where I will forward specific technical questions related to the book.

When you write, please be sure to include this book's title and author as well as your name, email address, and phone number. I will carefully review your comments and share them with the author and editors who worked on the book.

Email: feedback@quepublishing.com

Mail: Greg Wiegand
           Associate Publisher
           Que Publishing
           800 East 96th Street
           Indianapolis, IN 46240 USA

Reader Services

Visit our website and register this book at quepublishing.com/register for convenient access to any updates, downloads, or errata that might be available for this book.

Introduction

Welcome to Bento

The Database for the Rest of Us

Bento is a product from FileMaker, which is owned by Apple. Designed to bring FileMaker's database expertise to users of Mac OS X Leopard and later, it integrates data from iPhoto, iCal, Mail, and Address Book with databases that you can create from your own data as well as data imported from other sources.

Bento is lightweight in its structure but heavyweight in its capabilities. Because it builds on so many years' (actually decades') worth of experience with users and their needs both at FileMaker and at Apple, it is responsive to the frequently expressed needs and frustrations of people who need more organization than a word processing document or spreadsheet can provide but less complexity than a full-featured multiuser database might provide. Organization is the key to making information usable. A few items that are organized (ideas, recipes, addresses, bills, or shoes) can be more useful than a thousand items that are scattered around helter-skelter with no organization scheme.

Released in beta in the fall of 2007 and in a final version in early winter 2008, Bento caught on immediately. The response was positive both in reviews and in user comments. Because the Bento team is so agile and also because its design is so simple yet sophisticated, it was possible to produce a second version of the software within a year.

The Bento team did not rest on their laurels. They continued to work hard, incorporating new features as well as important advances elsewhere in Mac OS X and in the world of computing. Hard on the heels of Bento 2, the team released the Bento iPhone app (available for download from the iTunes App store). Together with Bento 2.5, which was a free upgrade, the Bento iPhone App lets you carry your Bento data around with you.

As the people at Apple worked on Snow Leopard (Mac OS X version 10.6), the Bento team worked to use new features to deepen the integration of Bento with the rest of the Mac environment. And in perhaps the most significant advance in Bento 3, it now is able to share data with up to five other computers on a local area network. Together with the Bento iPhone app and Apple's MobileMe service, this can mean that your data is always at your fingertips no matter where you are and what device you are using. Then, in the Spring of 2010, the Bento team delivered the Bento iPad app providing yet another perspective on your Bento data.

How This Book Is Organized

This book shows you how to use Bento and presents a number of projects that you can use (with or without modification). The projects are designed to illustrate the types of tasks that you can perform with Bento. You may choose to mix and match features and functionality from various projects to create your own solutions.

The general structure of the book is as follows:

- In the first few chapters, you see how to use the built-in Bento libraries.
- Next, you see how to customize them.
- Then you see how to import data from another source, such as a spreadsheet.
- Finally, you see how to create and share libraries for data you enter from scratch.

Along the way, the chapters explore various combinations of these techniques. Here is a summary of the chapters in the book:

- Chapter 1, "Bento: The Database for the Rest of Us," provides an introductory overview of Bento. It shows how you can organize your data, and it describes the basic Bento terminology, which consists of just four words. You see how to use the Bento window in both versions and how to set preferences.
- Chapter 2, "Using the Bento Window," uses the built-in Notes library to show you how to add and delete records, enter data, and find what you are looking for (both using a simple and advanced find technique).
- Chapter 3, "Working with Bento Forms," uses the built-in Classes library to explore how you can customize libraries with themes, columns, labels, shading, text size, and text boxes.
- Chapter 4, "Building a Bento Library from Your Own Data," provides a quick overview of how to import data from another source such as a spreadsheet. This topic is explored in more depth in Chapter 14, "Importing and Exporting Bento Data and Libraries."
- Chapter 5, "Working with Phone, URL, IM, and Address Fields and Lists in Contacts," explores the built-in Contacts library. You see how to use multiple forms and how to work with lists of phone numbers, URLs, addresses, emails, and IMs as well as how to add fields to a form.
- Chapter 6, "Working with Bento Fields and Calculations," shows how you can use calculation fields to make your data entry faster and more accurate. The built-in Exercise Log serves as the example.

- Chapter 7, "Expanding the Inventory Library with Related Records and Collections," delves into the concept of related records. You see how to take the built-in Inventory library and modify it so that it reflects additions or subtractions to or from inventory in a live, on-hand value.

- Chapter 8, "Synchronizing with the Bento iPhone and iPad Apps," shows you how to set up your iPhone and iPad and your Bento libraries for most effective synchronization.

- Chapter 9, "Sharing Data with Other Bento Users," shows you how to configure Bento for use over a local area network.

- Chapter 10, "Using Built-In Bento Libraries for Address Book and iPhoto," explores one of the most powerful parts of Bento: its integration with Address Book in Mac OS X. Bento accesses the Address Book data, and it is always live in the Bento display as well as in the Address Book display. You also see how this ties into MobileMe so that the data in Bento and Address Book is automatically synchronized with data elsewhere in your computing environment. The same interfaces and technologies that allow Address Book integration allow you to integrate Bento with your iPhoto library.

- Chapter 11, "Using Built-In Bento Libraries for iCal Tasks and Events," continues to look at how Bento is automatically integrated with your data on Mac OS X. This time, the iCal data is considered.

- Chapter 12, "Working with Bento's Projects Library to Use Related Records from iCal Tasks, iCal Events, and Address Book," shows how the built-in Bento Projects library uses the technologies described in Chapters 7, 10, and 11. Related records from the built-in Mac OS X applications are associated with specific projects. This allows integration so that, for example, iCal can display tasks and events over a period of time and across many projects while you can view each project separately in Bento. Furthermore, the integration of iCal and Address Book with MobileMe means that your Bento tasks, events, and contacts are automatically available on all your synchronized devices from Macs to PCs to iPhones. This chapter also shows the feature that lets you integrate messages from Mail with your Bento libraries.

- Chapter 13, "Designing a Projects Library to Share on Your LAN and Synchronize with Your iPhone," shows how you can customize the built-in Projects library with structured notes. This capability allows you to enter and browse comment and note data by date or other categories. Notes differ from tasks and events not only in that they are stored totally in Bento, not in iCal, but also because notes are a record of what has happened and been discussed in a project—the past, as well as the future events and tasks. For many people, this library may be all the project tracking they need.

- Chapter 14, "Importing and Exporting Bento Data and Libraries," explores Bento data import and export. You also see how to create and use your own Bento library templates.

- Chapter 15, "Using the Bento Template Exchange" shows you how to make the most of the shared templates available online and how you can contribute you own templates for others to use.

Using This Book

This book allows you to customize your own learning experience. The step-by-step instructions in the book give you a solid foundation in using FileMaker Bento, while rich and varied online content, including video tutorials and audio sidebars, provide the following:

- Demonstrations of step-by-step tasks covered in the book

- Additional tips or information on a topic

- Practical advice and suggestions

- Direction for more advanced tasks not covered in the book

Here's a quick look at a few structural features designed to help you get the most out of this book.

NOTE
Notes provide additional commentary or explanation that doesn't fit neatly into the surrounding text. Notes give detailed explanations of how something works, alternative ways of performing a task, and other tidbits to get you on your way.

TIP
This element gives you shortcuts, workarounds, and ways to avoid pitfalls.

CAUTION
Every once in a while there is something that can have serious repercussions if done incorrectly (or rarely, if done at all). Cautions give you a heads-up.

*⊙ **Cross-references:** Many topics are connected to other topics in various ways. Cross-references help you link related information together, no matter where that information appears in the book. When another section is related to one you are reading, a cross-reference directs you to a specific page in the book on which you can find the related information.*

 LET ME TRY IT tasks are presented in a step-by-step sequence so you can easily follow along.

 SHOW ME video walks through tasks you've just got to see—including bonus advanced techniques.

 TELL ME MORE audio delivers practical insights straight from the experts.

Special Features

More than just a book, your USING product integrates step-by-step video tutorials and valuable audio sidebars delivered through the **Free Web Edition** that comes with every USING book. For the price of the book, you get online access anywhere with a web connection—no books to carry, content is updated as the technology changes, and the benefit of video and audio learning.

About the USING Web Edition

The Web Edition of every USING book is powered by **Safari Books Online**, allowing you to access the video tutorials and valuable audio sidebars. Plus, you can search the contents of the book, highlight text and attach a note to that text, print your notes and highlights in a custom summary, and cut and paste directly from Safari Books Online.

To register this product and gain access to the Free Web Edition and the audio and video files, go to **quepublishing.com/using**.

Downloadable Files and Web Support

For updates to the book, see the author's website, www.northcountryconsulting.

Downloadable files for this book are available on the Web at:

- www.northcountryconsulting.com
- quepublishing.com/using

FileMaker is the developer of Bento. There are a number of resources on the FileMaker site:

- www.filemaker.com/bento gets you to the basic Bento page.
- There is a discussion forum for Bento at http://forums.filemaker.com/fmbnto/.

Bento: The Database for the Rest of Us

In this chapter you'll find an overview of Bento along with a step-by-step guide to getting started and understanding Bento's terminology.

Introducing Bento

Built on Mac OS X, Bento is a personal database from FileMaker. A wholly owned subsidiary of Apple, FileMaker has sold more than 15 million units of easy-to-use database software, to companies large and small as well as education, government, and research organizations. FileMaker's long-standing presence in the database world and the company's key understanding of how users use—and don't use—databases is how Bento has seen the success it has. At the same time, Bento is made possible not just by Apple's Mac OS X operating system, but also by Apple's decades of experience in how people use—and want to use—computers and other devices such as the iPod, iPhone, and now iPad.

When you first launch Bento, you will find yourself in an environment you already know because it uses the same specific interface elements from applications such as iPhoto, iCal, and iTunes, so what you see when it opens is just your basic Mac OS X application interface. Why should you have to work differently if you are dealing with photos or with music or with appointments? If you want to move a chair from one side of the room to another, you do it the same way in which you move a plant from one windowsill to another. (But you are still going to need help with that sofa.)

Looking at Bento

A quick look at Bento can provide a tantalizing view of the sorts of things that await you when you start to use it. Later in this book you will find ideas about how to use it productively as well as many details about the features that are available. For now, just take a look at Bento in action.

Figure 1.1 shows the basic Bento window. You will find out more about it in Chapter 2, "Using the Bento Window," but for now just look at the broad outlines.

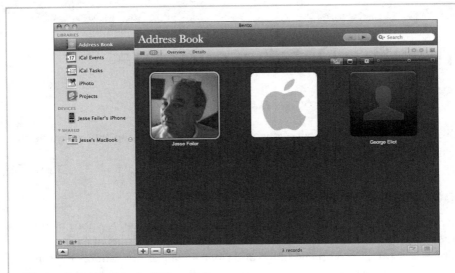

Figure 1.1   *Look at the Bento window.*

The most important part to notice is the libraries pane, at the left. This is where the libraries of Bento are shown (all data is stored in libraries). In Figure 1.1, notice some of the built-in libraries that come with Bento. Right out of the box, your iCal Events and Tasks, your Address Book, and your iPhoto library can be accessed from Bento.

Beneath these libraries, notice that Figure 1.1 shows both an iPhone and a separate computer (in this case a MacBook Pro). This integration is built into Bento.

If you click the MacBook Pro listing in the library pane, you will see the libraries available on that computer, as shown in Figure 1.2.

In Figure 1.3, notice two new libraries in the libraries pane: JF Projects and To Do Items. You can create your own libraries for your data. If you look at the center of the window shown in Figure 1.3, you can see that the To Do Items library is shown within the JF Projects libraries. (This is now a *form* view—it shows a single record from inside a library that is selected in the Libraries pane.) In fact, the JF Projects library is a new library that you can create; To Do Items is a library that is part of Bento. You can relate libraries to one another; a project can have any number of libraries associated with it. You can mix and match your own libraries and Bento-provided libraries to produce your own customized database. Organizing your data within libraries and with relationships between libraries lies at the heart of Bento as you will see later in this book.

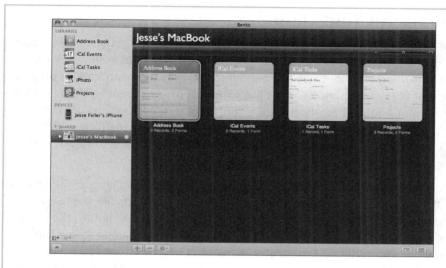

Figure 1.2   *View Bento libraries on other Macs on your local area network.*

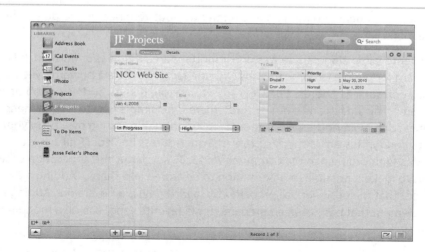

Figure 1.3   *Create your own libraries.*

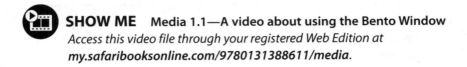

SHOW ME   Media 1.1—A video about using the Bento Window
Access this video file through your registered Web Edition at
my.safaribooksonline.com/9780131388611/media.

It's All About Your Data

What is it about your computer—your *personal* computer—that you value most? If it is from Apple, the sophisticated design of the hardware and intuitive look-and-feel of the interface might come to mind first. You may have applications on your computer that you simply could not live without: For some people, life is unthinkable without Adobe Photoshop or InDesign; for others, it is Quicken or Microsoft Excel; and for many Mac users, the components of iLife (iPhoto, iTunes, iWeb, iDVD, and Garage Band) or those of iWork (Numbers, Keynote, and Pages) are the indispensables.

But it is your data—and not these applications—that is generally most valuable to you: the list of your friends and colleagues inside your contacts file, the bills and payments in your accounting software, the music in your music library, the papers you have written for school, and the contracts you have prepared for your business. These are the items that you protect with frequent backups using technologies such as Time Machine, MobileMe, and iSync as well as external backups as needed.

Apple has been a leader in making information accessible. Address Book and Apple Mail share data easily; tools such as Services, AppleScript, and Automator make it easy to create complex tasks such as moving data from a FileMaker database to an InDesign document and then on to a printer without your needing to do anything more than click a mouse.

Until Bento came along, there was one important area that was unfinished. It is very hard for people to come to grips with the fact that while a powerful yet simple application such as Address Book lets you easily store names, addresses, job titles, nicknames, birthdays, and even pictures, there is no simple way to store a friend's favorite song in an Address Book record—even though the song may be in your iTunes library. This isn't a specific problem with Address Book or iTunes; it is a decades-long problem in the computer world. By and large, the application designer has to make it possible for information to be stored and shared. Adding a data element that the designer has prepared for (a birthday) is a no-brainer. Adding a data element that has not been prepared for (a favorite song) can be a monumental task.

Not only is it difficult to add new data elements to existing applications, it is also often extremely difficult to get information out of the walled fortresses that many applications seem to be. (Although Services, AppleScript, and Automator are an enormous help, not every application supports them.) That is why many people have a list of names and addresses in Address Book, another such list in an accounting program, yet another in a project management database, and so on.

Bento's Three Roles

Bento provides three related roles to help you address your data needs:

- Bento lets you store data.

- Bento integrates data from other Mac OS X apps.

- Bento lets you add fields to data from other apps.

First, Bento lets you store data—any data—in a database of your own. Regardless of whether it is a household inventory, guests at a party, or minutes of a meeting, you can store it in Bento.

But Bento goes beyond that. It gives you access to data from Address Book and iCal that is already on your computer as well as messages, notes, and RSS articles from Mail. This is not a copy of the data: it is the Address Book and iCal data itself. Make a change in Address Book to someone's phone number, and you see the changed number immediately in Bento. There is only one place where the data is stored, but Bento can see it and update it. (In the case of Mail messages, you can view messages in Bento and then click to edit them in Mail.)

Similarly, Bento can access media and other files on your computer. As with Address Book and iCal data, this data remains where it is, but Bento can display it.

Finally, Bento solves the favorite-song issue. You can view Address Book data in Bento, selecting the editable fields that you want displayed. You set the format and layout of the data. And if you want that favorite song, you can add it to your Bento data display so that it integrates both Address Book data and your added data in the form of a song. When you are looking at Bento, you do not see that some of the data comes from Address Book and other data (the favorite song, for example) comes from somewhere else. It is all together in Bento, just as you want it to be.

If you want to organize your data your way, Bento is for you. Bento is not about figuring out where your data is or how it is stored. It's about what data you want to see and how you want to see it. "Seeing" in this sense means more than just viewing it: You can change it in Bento, and it is changed wherever it is stored, whether that is inside Bento itself or in iCal, Address Book, or Mail.

So that is what Bento is—a personal database for your data, organized and displayed just the way you want it, without your worrying about anything else.

Bento Lets You Leap Over Boundaries

As a personal database, Bento enables you to combine your information, be it in Bento itself, in Mail, Address Book, or iCal. That means all your data is in one place—on your Mac—and you can use it as you see fit. But Bento 3 does much more—it makes your data as mobile as you are! It is your data, and, with Bento 3, it is where you are. Bento 3 not only integrates your Address Book and iCal data, but it also can synchronize your data with your iPhone. The Bento iPhone and iPad apps, (downloadable from the iTunes App Store for $4.99) means that you can keep your Mac and iPhone data in sync, even allowing you to decide what data is synchronized and what is not. More about this topic can be found in Chapter 8, "Synchronizing with the Bento iPhone and iPad Apps."

You can share data even beyond your Mac and your iPhone and iPad by sharing your libraries over a local area network with up to five other Bento users (more on this in Chapter 9, "Sharing Data with Other Bento Users").

And there's more if you use Apple's MobileMe service, which enables you to synchronize iCal and Address Book data with other Macs across the Internet. If you synchronize data with a server such as Entourage, your data can find its way into other databases—subject, of course, to your security settings.

For many people, their Bento libraries become the hub of their personal data; they use Bento as their primary interface to join the data together in whatever way is most convenient. You do not have to use all of these options. You can construct your own personal database from any of these tools: Bento (the hub), your iPhone, up to five Macs on your local area network, MobileMe and people to whom you have granted access, and also to Entourage. You can add or subtract components as you wish. And rest assured that if you simply want to use Bento on your Mac without any of these interfaces, you can do so and still have a remarkably powerful and customizable tool.

How Much Programming Does Bento Require?

There is a one-word answer to the question of how much programming Bento requires: none. Programming generally requires you to describe the processes that you want to have happen. (It is frequently called *procedural programming*.) Although the terminology is different, it is similar to writing out a set of instructions for a recipe or for changing a tire. Do this, then do that, and then.... The sequence ("then") is important.

In Bento and some other modern databases, you don't have to worry about the recipe; you just create the structure of your data from a real-world point of view—not a programmer's point of view. An entry in your Address Book can have a name and an address; it also (in your Bento version) can have a favorite song for that person. There is no sequential process for manipulating the data. For example, in Bento, you could find all your friends whose favorite song is *Summertime*. Or you could go the other way and find the favorite songs of all your friends who live in Denver.

All Bento asks is that you think about how the data is related to itself, and that is a simple process.

What Does "Personal" Mean?

The Bento environment exists for each user on a given computer. If you share a computer, your account has its own Bento database, and other accounts on that computer (perhaps for other members of your family) have their own Bento databases. If you do not share your computer, you still have an account, but it may not be obvious to you. Go to File > System Preferences and select Accounts. You see the window shown in Figure 1.4.

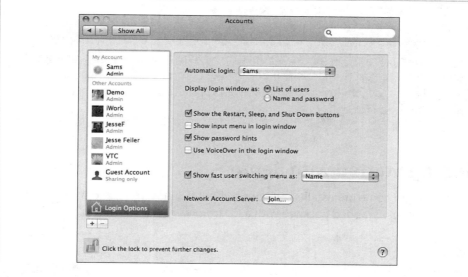

Figure 1.4   *Create accounts and manage automatic login from System Preferences.*

Login Options at the lower left of the window brings up the options shown at the right of the window. If Automatic Login is enabled, it is set at the top of those options. (To change the options, you need to unlock the window by clicking the padlock icon in the lower left corner of the window and supplying an administrator password.) In the default Mac OS X installation, a single user account is created, and it is set to automatically be logged in, so you might not realize that you have your own account—but you do. If you have multiple accounts on the computer, you can select one for automatic login. If you want to disable it, use the pop-up menu to set it to Off rather than to an account name. (This is a more secure setting, particularly if the computer is in a public place.)

You can also use this window to create other accounts on your computer. If you are sharing the computer, it is possible that you have been doing so just by organizing folders for each member of the household. It is preferable to go to System Preferences and create separate accounts for each user. In that way, each user is able to set his or her preferences for various features. Because Bento stores a user's database in a specific location inside that user's account, only one Bento database can exist for each user. (That is why using folders within a single account works for documents that you can move around, but it does not work for Bento.)

TIP

If you have separate folders for various users within your own account, you can easily create accounts for them as described previously, and you can let them copy their files from folders in your account to their new accounts. Simply move those folders (properly named, of course) to your Public folder. Then when a new user logs in, he can find your Public folder if he goes to the hard disk and then selects the Users folder, the name of your account, and then the Public folder. From there, the user can drag the appropriate folder into his own Documents (or other) folder.

Getting Started with Bento

Bento might come preinstalled on your computer. If not, you can download it or order a shrink-wrapped package with a CD from www.filemaker.com.

TIP

Because Bento can access data from Address Book and iCal as well as from Mail, it will help you if you have some data in Address Book and iCal as well as Mail. If you have not used Address Book or iCal, you might want to enter a little data in them: Two addresses for Address Book and two each of iCal Tasks (To Dos) and iCal Events (specific dates and times) will suffice.

When you first launch Bento, you see the Home dialog, as shown in Figure 1.5. You can watch a movie about Bento or get started either by creating a new library or selecting Start Using Bento.

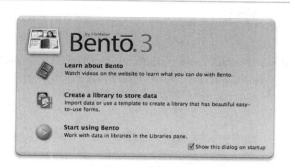

Figure 1.5   *Use the Home dialog the first time you launch Bento.*

You can always reopen this dialog with Window > Home. Use Bento > Preferences to open the Preferences dialog shown in Figure 1.6. In the When Bento Starts section of the dialog, you can control whether the Home dialog is shown each time you launch Bento.

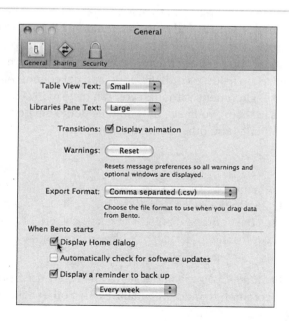

Figure 1.6   *Use Preferences to control whether Bento displays the Home dialog at startup.*

You can set up Bento for Address Book or iCal at any time by selecting File > Address Book, iCal, and iPhoto Setup.

 SHOW ME   Media 1.2—A video about setting Bento preferences
Access this video file through your registered Web Edition at
my.safaribooksonline.com/9780131388611/media.

> **NOTE**
> This chapter covers the basics of Bento—later in the book you find step-by-step walk-throughs describing how to create your own Bento libraries. In this overview, the focus is on what to do and how to talk about Bento and the interface elements in the Bento window. The screenshots are taken from various Bento templates that you will find installed for you. The different screenshots are designed to give you an idea not only of what you can do with Bento, but also what it can look like. In later chapters, you see how to create your own libraries and customize the Bento templates.

Understanding Bento Terminology

Like all databases, Bento enables you to manage data. Data can be of various types: text, numbers, graphics, videos, and music. In addition, Bento lets you treat files, folders, and email messages on your Mac as data. Databases help you organize data, and in doing so, you need to structure that data. In Bento, the data structuring is simple. It relies on fields, records, libraries, and collections. All of them exist within your Bento environment. Although you can have many libraries (containing records with fields in them), you have only a single Bento environment that includes all your libraries and other Bento entities.

> **NOTE**
> Your Bento environment is located inside your Home folder in Library > Application Support > Bento. Do not move or rename this folder. Launch Bento, and it automatically opens the appropriate file. In general, stay out of the Library folder unless you are absolutely certain of what you are doing.

In the sections that follow, you will find ways to effectively use fields and records, concepts that are common to modern databases. Two other concepts—libraries and collections—are specific to Bento.

Fields

A field contains a single data element such as a phone number or a picture. In Bento, it can be a file or folder, and that object itself can contain more data. References to email messages in Mail can also be stored in fields.

🄖 *This section provides an overview of Bento's fields. For more information about creating fields and working with the Fields dialog, **see** Chapter 6, "Working with Bento Fields and Calculations," p. 87.*

Each field in Bento has a name and a *type*, such as text, number, or checkbox. A person's weight is a number; that person's name is text. Bento defines several field types that are common to many databases. Several of the fields have options that you can set, such as the number of decimal places and whether to use a thousands separator in a number field. To define fields and set their options, you use the Fields dialog, shown in Figure 1.7 and described more fully in Chapter 6. The names of fields must be unique in the library. (Libraries are described later in this section.)

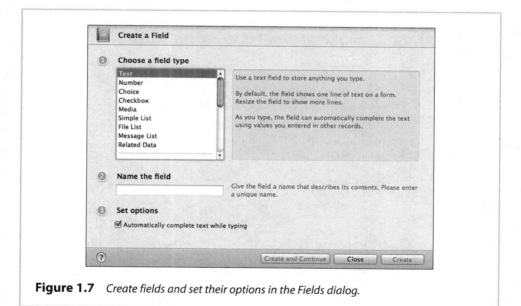

Figure 1.7 *Create fields and set their options in the Fields dialog.*

You can change a field's type after you create it. Bento converts existing data to the new type. Because not all field types can be converted to all other field types, Bento shows you only the types to which a given field can be converted.

Bento's formatting of fields is based on the settings you provide in System Preferences in Mac OS X. In the Language & Text pane, you can select the language you prefer by dragging it to the top of the list of languages shown in the Language tab. Use the Formats tab to set the formats to be used for that language. In Figure 1.8 you can see different settings for English/U.S. and French/Switzerland.

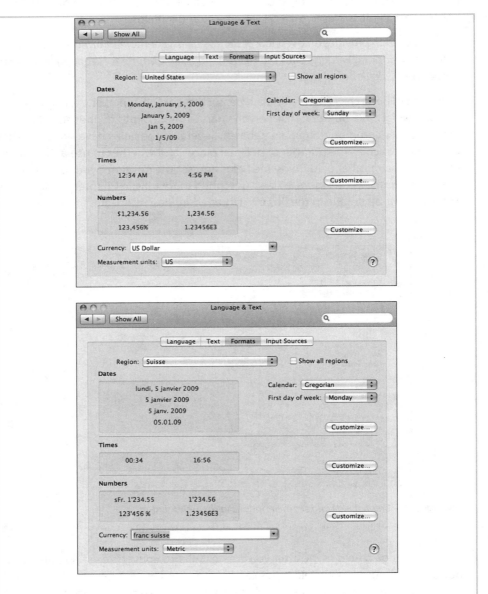

Figure 1.8 *International formatting preferences for English/U.S. (top) and French/Switzerland (bottom).*

NOTE

In the Fields dialog (see Figure 1.4), you have a checkbox option to set whether or not to use the thousands separator in displaying a number. What that thousands separator (a comma, dot, or space) separates is determined in the Formats tab of the International pane of System Preferences.

It is important to note that Mac OS X presents data in various ways regardless of how the underlying data is formatted. Applications generally store dates, numbers, and currency values in format-neutral ways. They then present that data to Mac OS X, which applies the selected International format options. Bento continues from there in the field types described in the following section:

- *Text* is for any text ranging from nothing to several lines of text.

- *Number* is a number of any kind.

- *Currency* is for monetary values. You can set the currency type, whether negative numbers are shown in parentheses or with a minus sign, and whether they are highlighted. You can also determine the alignment (right or left -justified) of the value. Finally, you can set the currency symbol. This is based on the International Format preferences, but you can refine it for specific fields in Bento, which lets you display one or more values in other than your default currency.

- *Time* contains hour and minute values. When you create the field, you can indicate that it is displayed as a Short format (no seconds) or a Medium format (including seconds).

- A *duration* field stores a period of time; depending on how detailed you want the duration to be, the field can contain weeks, days, hours, minutes, and seconds either as full words or as their one-letter abbreviations (w, d, h, m, s).

- *Date*. There are three sets of options you can set. The first lets you display Month and Year or Month, Day, and Year. The second lets you choose the format—Short (9/25/2008), Medium (Sep 25, 2008), Long (September 25, 2008), or Full (day, September 25, 2008). Finally, you can click a checkbox to add the time to the display—either in Short or Medium format as described previously in the time field.

- A *media* field is used to store a picture, movie, or sound (music). If your Mac includes a camera, Bento lets you use it so that you can capture a picture or movie and store it directly in Bento.

In addition, Bento has several field types that are designed not only to store data, but also to present it in special ways on the interface:

- A *choice* field has a list of values that you specify when you create the field. They are presented as a popup menu, and the user can choose a single value.

- A *checkbox* field has a name, and it is presented with that name and a checkbox. The user can select or deselect the checkbox indicating whether the checkbox value is true or false. Note that this meaning of "checkbox" is different from the basic Mac interface meaning where more than one value can be checked.

- A *rating* field has a value from 1 to 10. (You can set the range that is allowed.) When it is displayed in Bento, the appropriate number of stars is shown, and you can highlight how many are to be used in the rating (3 out of 5, for example).

- An *automatic counter* is an automatically generated number for each record that is created. It is unique for each record in a library; you can specify its starting value and the amount by which it is to be incremented. Normally, both of those values are 1. You will see how to use a counter in Chapter 6.

- An *encrypted* field lets you store data such as passwords in a secure way. This is a new feature in Bento 3; you find out more about it in Chapter 6, "Working with Bento Fields and Calculations."

Next, there are four list field types that let you present multiple items in a single scrolling list field.

- A *file list* field contains aliases to files. Double-clicking an item in the file list field opens that file using the default application for that file or file type.

- A *related data* field contains records that you have selected from another Bento library. You can click a button to go to a selected related record; from there you can click another button to return to the initial record.

   Ⓖ *There is more information on related records in Chapter 7, "Expanding the Inventory Library with Related Data Fields and Collections," p. 107.*

- A *message list* field contains email messages, RSS articles, and notes from Mail.

- A *simple* list displays data in a spreadsheet-like table with row and column headings.

As is the case with many databases, you can create calculation field types: they store the result of a calculation that often involves the data from other fields. If you have a field called temp_farenheit that contains the temperature in Farenheit, you can create a calculation field called temp_celsius that calculates the appropriate value. Calculations can also include values such as today's date that are not stored in fields. Furthermore, calculations can produce results that are themselves a text value or a number, date, time, duration, or currency. For example, if you have separate fields for first and last names, you can create a calculation field to combine them and to insert a space between them.

Lastly, there are five complex data types you can use. These combine several fields in a single data structure. For example, the address data type provides space for several addresses along with a label (home, work, other, or a custom label) for each one.

- Address

- Phone Number

- Email Address

- URL

- IM Address

⊙ *You will see how to use these complex data types in Chapter 5, "Working with Phone, URL, IM, and Address Fields and Lists in Contacts," p. 77; calculations are covered in Chapter 6, "Working with Bento Fields and Calculations," p. 87.*

Records

Bento data is stored in fields, and the fields are stored in *records*. Each record within a Bento library contains the same fields, although the values are different. A record often corresponds to a real-life entity: a student, an inventory item, or a motion at a meeting. The record's fields could be name and class for a student, price and size for an inventory item, or wording and result of a vote for a resolution.

When you think about your Bento data, you can envision it as a table or spreadsheet with the columns representing fields and the rows representing records. If your data does not fit into that type of tabular structure, you may need to rethink it. For example, if you want to keep track of all your data—your bank accounts, your favorite songs, your photos, your friends, important dates to remember for your family, and your family tree—you can see that set of data does not lend itself to the row/column structure. But there is a solution. Because Bento lets you relate data to other data in your Bento database, you can split up your data into substructures that are two-dimensional: a list of bank accounts, list of songs, list of photos, and so forth. Each of these sets of records and their fields make a neat two-dimensional table, and you can combine them in Bento into a composite view of your data.

When it comes to database design, "divide and conquer" is often a good strategy. Furthermore, putting too much together into a too complex data structure is often a dead-end route. Start small and use Bento to help join your component parts together.

☞ *Bringing data together involves creating relationships. You can find more about this topic in Chapter 7, "Expanding the Inventory Library with Related Data Fields and Collections," p. 107.*

Libraries

A *library* is a set of records in Bento. As noted previously, you have a single Bento environment, but you can have many libraries within it. When you launch Bento for the first time, normally you have several libraries that are already created from your Address Book, iCal, and iPhoto data. You can create other libraries from Bento templates or build them yourself from scratch.

☞ *For more on Bento's interface to Address Book, **see** Chapter 11, "Using Built-in Bento Libraries for iCal Tasks and iCal Events," p. 171. For the iCal interface, **see** Chapter 9, "Sharing Data with Other Bento Users," p. 145.*

Although from a data point of view, libraries contain records, they also contain interface elements, such as forms, which are described in Chapter 2, "Using the Bento Window."

Collections

The structure described so far is simple: Fields contain data elements, and fields are organized into records. Your libraries consist of records that you can add and delete as you add or delete data.

You can also create collections. These are collections of records within a library that you create using Bento. They are comparable to playlists in iTunes, albums in iPhoto, or groups in Address Book. They could be attendees at a meeting or inventory items that a specific customer purchases. Collections appear in the Source list underneath the library to which they belong. They are slightly indented, and their icons are a bit smaller than the library icon.

In Figure 1.9, you can see two collections that are part of the Inventory library (Sale Items and Smart Sale). This figure also shows the main records area of the window as a table or list rather than as a grid as shown previously.

Groups from Address Book (Friends, Business, and Personal) are shown in Bento as collections. As you will see later in this section, collections can be assembled manually, or they can be Smart Collections that are automatically created based on criteria that you set. The small triangle to the left of the library's icon lets you expand or contract the library so that its collections are or are not shown.

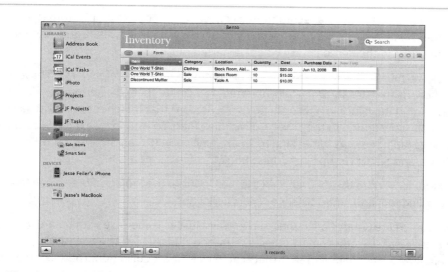

Figure 1.9   *You can organize a library's records into collections.*

Collections introduce one of the key elements of digital organization: Digital objects can be in more than one place at a time. In the physical world, a document is in one drawer of a file cabinet or another drawer. If you take it out and put it on your desk, it is no longer in the file cabinet. You can make a copy of the document and put the copy on your desk, but you now have two versions of the document. If you make a note on the copy on your desk, that note is on that copy but not on the original version of the document in the file cabinet.

In the digital world, this basic rule of physics does not apply. You can have a record located in a library in Bento. That much is like the physical world, and, in fact, the record can be in only one library.

But if you create a collection, you can add that record to the collection, and that has no effect on the original record. When you view the record through the collection, you are looking at the record in its own Bento library; you are not looking at a copy. If you change the record data while viewing it in a collection, that change immediately is reflected in the record that is part of the Bento library (because it is the same record).

You can add a given record to many collections. There are no limits to the number of collections in which a record can reside. No matter how many collections it is in, there is only one version of the record; any change that you make to it in any collection or in the original Bento library is reflected everywhere the record is shown. If you delete the record from the Bento library, it is deleted everywhere.

However, if you remove a record from a collection, you delete it only from that collection; it still exists in every other collection to which it was added, and, of course, it still exists in the Bento library where it started out.

As powerful as collections are, *Smart Collections* are even more powerful. These are collections that are automatically updated. You create them by setting up criteria based on data values in a record's fields. Any record that matches those criteria is automatically added to the Smart Collection. Smart Collections are directly comparable to Smart Folders in the Finder, Smart Playlists in iTunes, Smart Albums in iPhoto, and Smart Groups in Address Book.

In Figure 1.9, note the difference in the icons: Under the Projects library, Sale Items is a collection, and Smart Sale is a Smart Collection.

You can create Smart Collections in two ways, just as is the case with Smart Folders in Finder and the other smart objects throughout Mac OS X. The first way is to search for certain data and save that search as a Smart Collection. The second way is to choose File > New Smart Collection and specify the search to be used.

Thereafter, whenever a record is created that matches the criteria in the Smart Collection, it shows up in the Smart Collection. If the basic record from the library is deleted, it disappears from the Smart Collection. And if a data value changes that causes a record to no longer match the criteria, it disappears from the Smart Collection but remains in the library. By the same token, if a data value changes in a library record in such a way that the record is now valid for a Smart Collection, it appears in the Smart Collection.

As with collections, you can have as many Smart Collections as you want, and as many records can be in as many collections and Smart Collections as you want.

TIP

As you experiment with Smart Collections, you will find some of the power of Bento. After the Smart Collection is set up, records come and go automatically. As you continue working with Bento, you can think about Smart Collections as you are laying out your fields and records. By creating fields that lend themselves to being criteria for Smart Collections, you can make your Bento database more dynamic.

ⓖ *For more details on collections and Smart Collections, **see** Chapter 7, "Expanding the Inventory Library with Related Data Fields and Collections," p. 107.*

Using the Bento Window

You'll explore the Bento window with its Records area as well as its Libraries & Fields pane. This chapter also helps you work with Bento preferences.

Getting Around the Bento Window

Like iTunes and iPhoto, Bento has a single window that you work in. (By comparison, applications such as Keynote, Numbers, and Pages allow multiple windows to be open at a time.) Figure 2.1 shows the Bento window.

The window in this figure shows the Projects library, which is one of the templates included with Bento. Like most of the Bento templates, it is not only a template in Bento, but also an actual library with a multitude of data records so that you can explore Bento and its navigation.

In addition to the window frame, there are two main sections of the window: the *Records area* in the center and right displays data, and the *Libraries pane* at the left (including a Shared section if there are shared libraries for you to use as well as a section for devices such as an iPhone that are synchronized with Bento).

In the lower left area of the window, an arrow lets you show and hide the *Fields pane*, which appears below the list in the Libraries pane. The fields pane is shown in Figure 2.2

The library you select from the Libraries pane is the library that is shown in the Records area. If the Fields list is visible, it contains the fields for that library.

To create a new library, either choose File > New Library or use the Add a Library button (+) from the bottom of the Libraries pane. Either action lets you choose from Bento's templates for libraries, as shown in Figure 2.3. Note that if the Fields pane is shown, the Add a Library button is at the bottom of the Libraries pane and above the Fields pane, as you see in Figure 2.3.

When the New Library dialog has opened, you can select the template you want to use as shown in Figure 2.4.

The templates are organized into groups. Some templates appear in more than one. For more information, select the library template you are interested in with a single click. Information about it appears at the bottom of the New Library dialog.

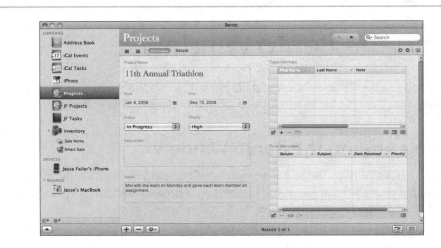

Figure 2.1   *Use the Bento window to manage your Bento data.*

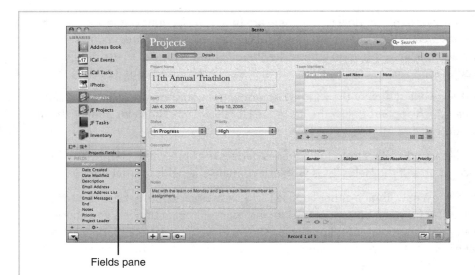

Fields pane

Figure 2.2   *Show or hide the Fields pane.*

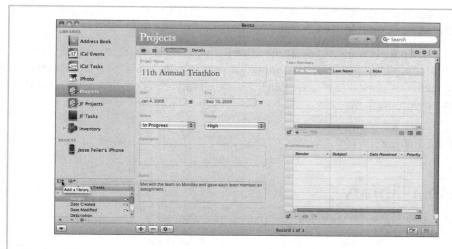

Figure 2.3   *Use the Add a Library button to add a new library.*

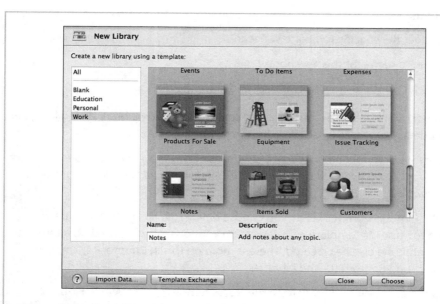

Figure 2.4   *Use the New Library dialog to create a library.*

The name of the library starts out as the name of the template, but the Name field is editable so that you can change it before you create it. When you have chosen the library you want, click Choose in the lower-right corner of the dialog to create it. Alternatively, double-click the library template to create it.

You can then look more closely at the library. If you realize that it is not quite what you are looking for, you can either modify it or try again. To delete a library, select it in the Libraries pane and choose Edit > Delete Library. You can also select it and delete it with the Delete key.

 **LET ME TRY IT**

Create a Library

Use the built-in Bento templates to create a new library.

1. Open the New Library dialog with one of these steps:

   a. Use the Add a Library button at the bottom of the Libraries pane.

   b. Choose File > New Library From Template.

2. In the New Library dialog, select the category of template you want to use.

3. Select the specific template you want.

4. Enter a name for the new library.

5. Click Choose to create the library and close the dialog.

The Import Data button in the lower-left corner of the New Library dialog lets you import data. You can also use File > Import to import data.

📎 *For more information on importing data, **see** Chapter 4, "Building a Bento Library from Your Own Data," p. 63 and Chapter 14, "Importing and Exporting Bento Data and Libraries," p. 213.*

The File > Import command lets you choose between a file and a template. If you choose to import a template, you can create your own library based on a template you or someone else has created. There is more on this in Chapter 14, "Importing and Exporting Bento Data and Libraries."

For now, create a Notes library from the Notes template, as shown in Figure 2.5. This library is selected because its data structure is as simple as possible. There are no collections and no related records, so it is a good place to start with Bento basics. (The Notes template is available in the Education, Work, and All categories.)

When you create a new Notes library, notice how each library template has a brief description in the lower right of the new template dialog that changes as you click on a template in which you might be interested.

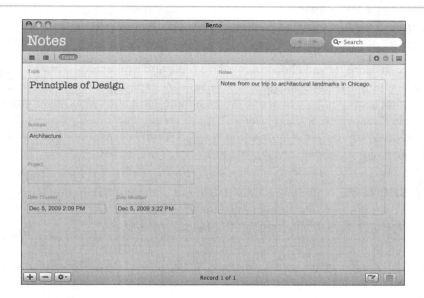

Figure 2.5   *Create a new library from the Notes template.*

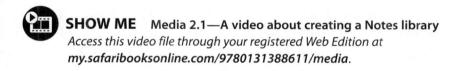

SHOW ME   Media 2.1—A video about creating a Notes library
Access this video file through your registered Web Edition at
my.safaribooksonline.com/9780131388611/media.

Using the Records Area

Having created a new library from a template, you will notice that a single record is present. You can confirm this by noting the Record 1 of 1 message at the bottom of the window. Some templates include several records as samples, but Notes contains only the one record. You can use the sample record as an example for further entries, you can modify its data, or you can delete it. For now, leave it as is.

You can choose View > Hide Libraries & Fields Pane to hide the Libraries and Fields panes if you want. That will leave you with only the records area showing.

Bento works within the size of its window, which you can resize in the normal way from the lower-right corner. If you choose to show only the Records area, the window retains its size, and the display of the Records area grows to fill the window.

The *navigation bar* at the top of the window provides the navigation and display controls for your data. It is in two sections. The upper one contains the library name, next and previous arrows, and a search field; these are discussed later in this chapter in the "Finding Data" section.

The lower portion of the navigation bar lets you control the display of your data. At the far left, icons let you choose between a table and a grid view—they let you browse multiple records at a glance. A vertical line separates them from the form views that allow you to look at one record at time. Each library has an automatically generated table view and a grid view; it must have at least one form view; the Notes library has only one form, and it is called Form. At the far right, icons let you create new forms as well as view data in split multiple formats.

 SHOW ME   Media 2.2—A video about using the Navigation Bar
Access this video file through your registered Web Edition at
my.safaribooksonline.com/9780131388611/media.

➔ *Find out more about creating forms in Chapter 3, "Working with Bento Forms," p. 49.*

Introducing Table Views

View records from your library in a *table view* by using the icon at the left of the bottom row of the navigation bar, View > Table View, or Command-1. As you can see in Figure 2.6, you can resize columns in the table view. Simply drag any of the column dividing lines to the right or left.

The spreadsheet-like display of data lets you see multiple records at a time. It can also make data entry much faster. There is more on table views later in this chapter.

Introducing Grid Views

The second icon from the left in the second row of the navigation bar displays the grid view as shown in Figure 2.7.

Like the table view, you can see multiple records at a time in the grid view. To illustrate the possibilities, a second record has been added to the library; you will see how to do that later on in this chapter.

By default, the grid view displays a thumbnail version of a form for the library. The images shown in the grid view in Figure 2.7 show the forms; as you can see in the second thumbnail, an image field has been added, and the image is visible instead of the form view.

Bento takes care of this for you automatically, but sometimes you want to customize the display. Controls at the top right of the grid view let you modify it. The left of the three buttons lets you view images from the records as shown in Figure 2.8.

Table view icon

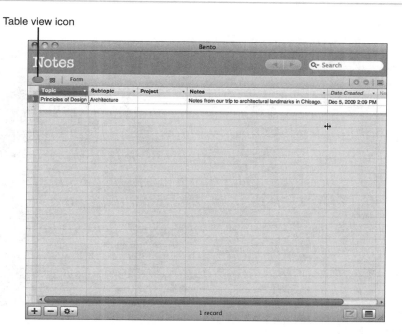

Figure 2.6　*Resize columns in a table view.*

If there are no images, defaults are displayed as shown in Figure 2.7. The second button shows the thumbnail view shown previously in Figure 2.6. When images are displayed, they fill the thumbnail, but if there is more than one in a record, as you move your mouse across the thumbnail you can browse through the images.

There is still more customization available to you. Use the Additional Commands button (the gear wheel) to bring up the settings shown in Figure 2.9.

You can also use the small arrow in the lower right of the image to select which of several image fields is used in the thumbnails. Finally, you can use the slider shown in Figure 2.8 to adjust the size of all thumbnails. (They must always be the same size in a grid view.)

Using Split Views

Both the table and grid views show you multiple records at a time. Forms show you a single record at a time.

You see how to create new forms and rename them in Chapter 3, "Working with Bento Forms," p. 49.

Grid view icon

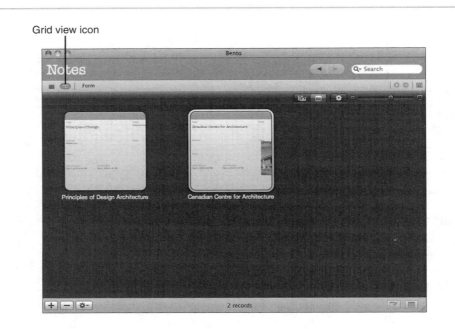

Figure 2.7   *View records in a grid view.*

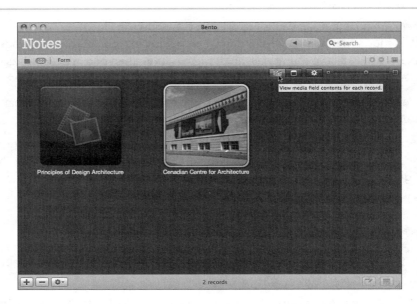

Figure 2.8   *Use grid view.*

Figure 2.9 *Customize grid view displays.*

Sometimes it is useful to see both a multiple-record view (a grid or table view) and a single record view (a form view) at the same time. Do that either with Views > Split View, Command-3 or the icon at the far right of the lower part of the navigation bar. A split view is shown in Figure 2.10.

You can drag the dividing line between the two views up and down so that you see more or less of each one. (The form view is always on the bottom.) Sometimes the multiple-record display of a table or grid view is more useful to you; other times, you need more space for the form view so that you can see all of a single record's data.

Creating a New Record

In form, grid, or table view, create a new record in any of these ways:

- Choose Records > New Record to create a blank record.

- Choose Records > Duplicate Record to duplicate a record; you can then modify the data. Use this technique if you need a record that is similar to an existing one.

- Use the Add a Record button (+) at the bottom of the Records area.

There is always a blank line at the bottom of the table view. You can just start to type your data there without using an explicit command. As soon as you click or tab out of the first field in which you have entered data, a new record with that data is created, and a new blank line below it appears in the table view.

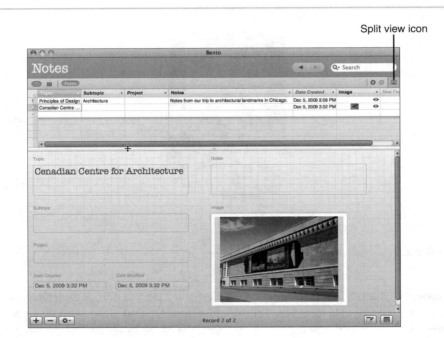

Figure 2.10 *Use the split view to see a table and form view together.*

When you create a new record in any of these ways, you see a nearly blank record. In the default Notes library, the Date Created field is filled in with the current date and time. This field is present in every Bento record (along with Date Modified). You can use these fields to search for records created or modified at certain times. You do not have to display the fields, but they can be useful for troubleshooting.

 SHOW ME Media 2.3—A video about creating a new record
Access this video file through your registered Web Edition at
my.safaribooksonline.com/9780131388611/media.

By default, you are in the first field, which in this case is Topic. You can tab from field to field: the order in a form is from top to bottom in the first column and then top to bottom in the second column. You cannot change the order, but you can move the fields so that they are entered in a logical sequence.

Ⓖ *For more information on changing the look of a form,* **see** *Chapter 3, "Working with Bento Forms," p. 49. For more information on changing the look of a table view,* **see** *the section "Using Table Views in Bento" later in this chapter.*

Entering Text Data

Enter text data by typing or by using the Clipboard to copy and paste it from else-where in Bento or anywhere else on your computer. Bento takes care of the format-ting automatically. You can do this in either form or table views.

There are a few special commands you can use to assist you in entering text data. To enter the current date and time, choose Insert > Current Date and Time. You can use this command in a date or time field as well as in a text field, and you can mod-ify the value (for example, to change today's date to a properly formatted date for tomorrow just by changing the day number).

 **LET ME TRY IT**

Using Spell Checking

When it comes to text data, you can use the built-in Mac OS X features that are available in the Edit > Spelling submenu. You can check spelling at any time; you can also choose to check spelling as you type.

1. Select the type of spell checking you want—either as you type or when you choose the command.

2. Experiment by misspelling a word. For example, in Figure 2.10, the word "Canadian" is misspelled.

3. Use the Edit > Spelling > Spelling command, which is what shows or hides the window shown at the front in Figure 2.11.

4. If the word is misspelled, you can correct it here (although you can do that simply by changing the highlighted word).

5. If it is spelled correctly, you can add it to your dictionary. Just like Bento, your dictionary is specific to your Mac OS X user account; if you add a word to your dictionary, it is added for any Mac OS X applications that use the built-in spelling feature.

TIP

Add words you use frequently to your dictionary and turn on Check Spelling While Typing for the best results. By adding your own commonly used words to your dictionary, you avoid warning of misspelled words that are actually correct-ly spelled but not in the default dictionary. By automatically flagging possible spelling errors (and minimizing false positives), you get in the habit of correcting words quickly.

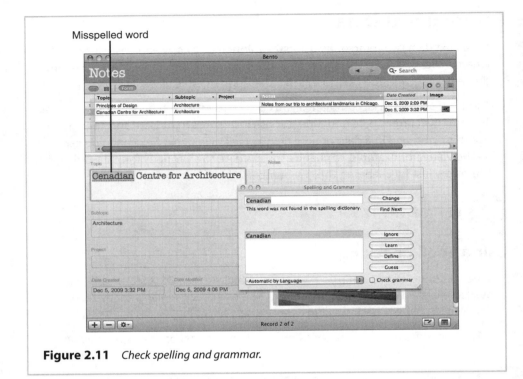

Figure 2.11   *Check spelling and grammar.*

As the book moves through different types of libraries in its examples, you will find details of entering data for other types of fields.

Printing a Record

Whether for a hard-copy backup or to share information with other people, you often need to print out Bento data. Choosing File > Print or Print from the Additional commands button at the bottom of the Records area does the trick. Either one brings up the dialog shown in Figure 2.12.

One thing you will notice immediately is that this dialog includes the orientation and page size settings that you are used to finding in a Page Setup command. The preview at the left of the dialog is live, so you can see how your settings affect the printed version of the data.

The most important settings are the radio buttons toward the center of the dialog that let you control whether all displayed records are to be printed or only the selected records. If you have searched for records, those are the selected records; if you are browsing a record, it is the only selected record. You can manually create a set of selected records in a table or grid view by selecting more than one record; as always, Shift-click the first and last records in a contiguous list and Command-click the various records in a noncontiguous list.

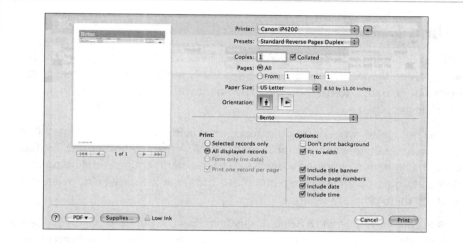

Figure 2.12   *Print Bento data.*

You can use this setting together with the page printing settings to determine what the total set of printable records is (with the radio buttons) and then which of those are to be printed.

In Bento 3, you now have an option to print a blank form. This allows you to print forms for people to fill in by hand. You can also use the PDF button at the lower left of the Print dialog to create PDF files; one of the menu choices is to mail a PDF file. That is a simple way to distribute a blank form to one or more people to fill in.

The checkboxes at the right of the dialog let you control the formatting of the print-out. One of the most important settings here is whether to print the background. Some elegant color combinations that work on the screen do not work well on printed copies—particularly if they are to be printed on a black-and-white printer, photocopied, or faxed. In those cases, you might not want to print the background.

TIP

You can print forms or table views; you cannot print grid views.

SHOW ME   Media 2.4—A video about printing records in Bento
Access this video file through your registered Web Edition at
my.safaribooksonline.com/9780131388611/media.

Finding Data

Before continuing with this chapter, enter at least two more records into the Notes library using the techniques described previously in this chapter. The reason for entering the data is so that you can experiment with finding and sorting data, which is described next.

It does not matter what data you enter or what fields you use. In the Notes library, you can enter unique names in the Topic field. ("Test" and "Another Test" are fine to use.) The limitation of unique names is only for experimenting with finding data. Bento has no problem handling multiple records with identical field values and keeping them properly separate.

↻ *In Chapter 4, "Building a Bento Library from Your Own Data," p. 63, you see how to import data into Bento. When you have mastered those techniques, you can use sample libraries and data from the book's website as described in the Introduction.*

Whether you are using form, grid, or table view, you can find data in your library. The simplest way of doing so is to type a word, phrase, or value into the search field at the upper right corner of the Bento window. Bento carries out the search as you type in the search field and shows you the number of records found, as you can see in Figure 2.13. The search is carried on against the data in the record. That is why in a grid view you may not be able see the field that matches the search as Figure 2.13 illustrates.

Bento handles data conversion for you automatically The bottom of the Bento window shows you how many records have been found. You can switch back and forth among form, grid, and table views; the records you have found remain. To see all records, delete the search criterion either by clicking the small round X in the search box or by deleting the text. (This is the same searching interface you find in Spotlight and other Mac OS X searches.)

> **NOTE**
> Summaries in table view reflect the records that have been found, not the entire set of records.

If you experiment with your test data, you will see that you can find whole words, parts of words, and even single characters within a word. You do not need to use special symbols to do this—it just happens.

Figure 2.13   *Search for data.*

Figure 2.13 shows another Bento feature that is available in form view. Arrows let you move to the next and previous record; they are located to the left of the search field. In most cases, using Find is faster than manually searching through the library with next and previous arrows unless you are dealing with structured data that is inherently sequenced (such as appointments by date or time) and that has been sorted.

Using Advanced Find

You can use Advanced Find to create more sophisticated searches. You go to Advanced Find either by choosing Records > Advanced Find or by clicking the small downward arrow next to the magnifying glass at the left of the search field. As you can see from Figure 2.14, that downward arrow brings up a contextual menu that lets you go to Advanced Search, repeat recent searches, or clear the search history.

Figure 2.15 shows the Advanced Find features. You may very well have seen them before in Spotlight, the Finder, and other applications. (Note that Figure 2.14 shows the Advanced Find as you might set it up and before you click the Find button.)

Starting from the top of the window shown in Figure 2.15, there are three sections of Advanced Find. They provide a compact and powerful interface to Bento's searching capabilities. You can set up several search criteria if you want; you also can make each of them more specific than the simple find mechanism described in the preceding section. (That is how, for example, you can find Another Test but not Test.)

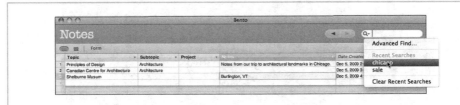

Figure 2.14   *Find more search options.*

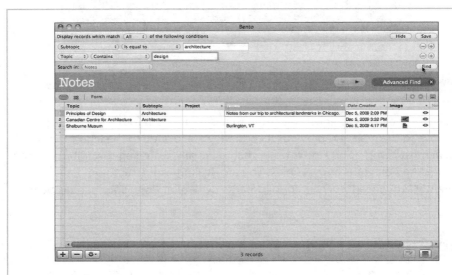

Figure 2.15   *Use Advanced Find.*

In the first row at the top of the window, you decide whether you want all the conditions to be applied or any of them. *All* (a logical *and* in database parlance) means that they all have to be true. *Any* (a logical *or*) means that if even one is true, the record is selected. In complex databases, more combinations can be set up: You can combine a set of conditions, all of which must be true with a second set in which any can be true, and you can further specify other types of logical operators. For Bento, however, these two logical operators are sufficient.

Next, you specify the conditions. Each condition is applied to a field, and, as shown in Figure 2.15, you can specify what the logical test is. Finally, you specify the value to be tested. To add more conditions, click the plus sign (+) at the right of the row; to remove a condition, click the minus sign (–).

Finally, you click Find at the bottom right of the Advanced Find section. The search is then carried out. At the top right, you can see that you can hide the Advanced Find section. This capability is useful if you need to check some data values in the Records pane. Particularly if your Advanced Find has a number of criteria, you may not be able to see as much data as you want. Hiding Advanced Find does not destroy your search criteria. When you show Advanced Find again, everything is still there.

At the upper right of the Advanced Find area, you can save your search. In fact, you create a Smart Collection that is based on the search. As you add (or delete) records in your library, the Advanced Find is applied to each record, and the Smart Collection always shows the results of the Advanced Find. This process is described in detail in Chapter 7, "Expanding the Inventory Library with Related Data Fields and Collections," p. 107.

Because of the speed of Bento's finds and because you can build such complex Advanced Find searches, it is a good idea to use those tools rather than repeatedly sorting and manually searching the data. There are several tips that can help you use Bento's find mechanism quickly and productively. Here are a few of them:

- Use the simplest search possible to start.

- Although sorting the entire library is often unnecessary, combine sorting with searches. If you have several hundred (or thousand) names in your Address Book, you can quickly search on a company name and last name to find the person you are looking for. But if you can't quite remember the name, try searching on the company name first and then sorting the results by last name. As long as the find is active (that is, until you clear it with the X at the right of the find search field), only the found records are displayed or sorted.

- Think about how you will be searching for data as you build your library. Many manufacturers and distributors identify their products with a stock-keeping unit (SKU) code. If you will be using a SKU, place it in its own field so that you can easily look it up. If you enter it as part of the name of the prod-uct, you may wind up accidentally retrieving the wrong data elements because sometimes a SKU is already part of a title as in "Handle for briefcase SKU1." The actual handle SKU might be SKU2.

Deleting a Record

To delete a record, select it in table view or display it in form view and choose Records > Delete Selected Record(s) or use the minus sign (–) button at the lower left of the Records area. (In table view, you can select several records for deletion at once.)

> **TIP**
>
> Make certain you really want to delete the data. When it is gone, it is gone forever, except for copies that you may have in Time Machine or your Bento backups. If you are cleaning up a Bento library and deleting a lot of data, it is an excellent idea to use the backup and exporting features described in Chapter 14, "Importing and Exporting Bento Data and Libraries," before you delete data.

    ☉ *In addition, you can use a Smart Collection as described in Chapter 7, "Expanding the Inventory Library with Related Records and Collections," to create the appearance of deleting data without actually deleting it.*

Using Table Views in Bento

Table views let you see more than one record at a time from the library you are using. This allows you to do a number of things that you cannot do in Form view when you are looking at one record at a time. There are three of these features:

- You can sort records based on the values in any column.

- You can summarize the data in one or more columns.

- You can paste data into multiple records and fields in table view. In addition, the small triangle at the top of each column in Bento lets you edit the table structure using a contextual menu, as shown in Figure 2.16.

You can resize columns by dragging the dividers in the title row. You can also change the order of the columns by dragging the titles left or right until the order is what you want.

Sorting a Table View in Bento

Although only one column at a time can be highlighted and sorted, previous sorts remain in place. Thus, you can do a two-level sort. For example, you can sort a First Name column and then sort a Last Name column to give you a table that is sorted by Last Name and First Name. You sort the columns in reverse order with the secondary sort such as First Name being the first one you perform. This procedure is simple, intuitive, and fast in Bento.

Sort Ascending
Sort Descending

Add Field Before
Add Field After

Duplicate Field
Edit Field...
Change To   ▶
Delete Field

Hide Field

Figure 2.16   *Use the contextual menu from the triangle at the top of each column data in table view to sort and edit the table and its data in Bento.*

 TELL ME MORE   **Media 2.5—A discussion about the issues with pasting data into table views**
Access this audio recording through your registered Web Edition at
my.safaribooksonline.com/9780131388611/media.

Pasting Data into Table View in Bento (Part 1)

In table views in Bento, there is always a blank row at the bottom of the records displayed. As soon as you type in the first field (whatever field it is), a new record in the library is created. If you are pasting a column of data from a spreadsheet into Bento, it creates as many records as are necessary to store the values in the spreadsheet column.

TIP
This behavior applies to tabular data copied from spreadsheets as well as from tables in word processing applications such as Pages and Microsoft Word. A table that is constructed from tabs, spaces, and other formatting symbols is not a table in this sense. A table is one that is constructed in Microsoft Word by using Table > Insert Table > Table or Table > Convert > Text to Table. In Pages, it is a table constructed with Insert > Table. Many other applications provide similar functionality.

Editing Fields with Table View in Bento

As you can see from the contextual menu shown in Figure 2.16, in addition to sort-ing a selected column, you can add or delete fields before or after the selected col-umn, hide or duplicate the field shown in the column, edit the field name, or change its type. These commands are also available in the Libraries & Fields pane; they are discussed in the "Using the Libraries and Fields Pane" section later in this chapter.

For now, what is important to note is that in table view in Bento, in addition to being able to create a new record in the blank row that is always visible, you can add fields in the table view. An extra column is always available at the right in the same way that an extra row is always visible at the bottom. After you tab out of this new field, a new column is created, and a new extra column appears to the right of the added column. (Added fields are visible in the table view as well as all forms view if you choose to use them.)

Pasting Data into Table View in Bento (Part 2)

If you select more than one column in a table or spreadsheet, you can paste the data into a table view in Bento. In the previous section, it was noted that if more rows are needed, they are automatically created. If your Bento list view needs more columns for the data, they, too, are created.

This means that in an extreme case, you can create a Bento library with one record and one field. You can then select an entire spreadsheet or table from Microsoft Word or Pages and paste it into that one field in the one record. Bento adds as many records and fields as it needs to accommodate all the data. You can then use the contextual menus to change field types and names.

Using the Libraries & Fields Pane

The Libraries and Fields panes can be combined into a Libraries & Fields pane in Bento. If it is shown at all, the Libraries pane is at the top of the Libraries & Fields pane at the left of the Bento window, as shown in Figure 2.17. If the Libraries & Fields pane is not shown, choose View > Show Libraries & Fields pane. You control whether or not the Fields list is shown at the bottom with the triangle in the lower-left corner of the window.

As you create a new library, it is added to the end of the list. You can rearrange libraries by dragging them up and down. As you will see in Chapter 7, you can create collections and Smart Collections that are based on libraries. They are shown beneath the library on which they are based; you can use the small disclosure trian-gle next to a library's icon to show or hide its collections.

Figure 2.17   *The Libraries pane in the Libraries & Fields pane shows the libraries in Bento.*

Using Library Folders

You can now create library folders to organize your libraries. Choose File > New Library Folder to begin the process, as shown in Figure 2.18.

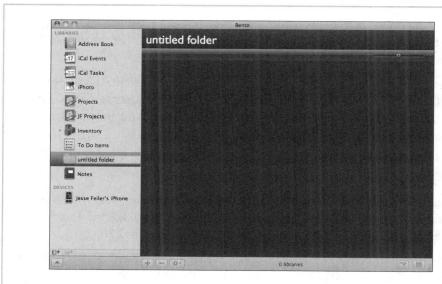

Figure 2.18   *Create a library folder.*

A new untitled folder is created for you. The first thing that you should do is to type in a new name (the field is selected in the library pane).

Drag libraries into your folder as shown in Figure 2.19.

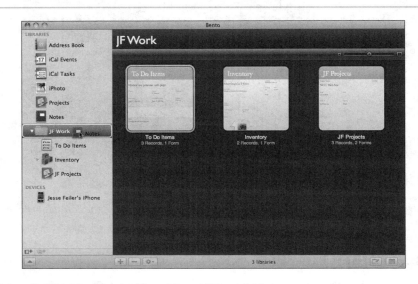

Figure 2.19   *Drag libraries into and out of library folders.*

Folders are only one level deep; you cannot have a folder within a folder. You can drag the libraries up and down within the folder, which changes the order in the display in the main part of the window.

Folders can be opened and closed with the triangles to their left. This lets you keep your Libraries pane clean by closing and opening library folders as well as libraries with their collections so that you can concentrate on what you are interested in at the moment.

Using Library Icons

You can choose from a variety of icons for your Bento libraries—both built-in libraries and those you create. In the Libraries pane, Control-click the library you are interested in to bring up the shortcuts menu shown in Figure 2.20.

Note that the shortcuts in this menu are all available from the menu bar with the exception of the last one: Choose a Library Icon. This is the only place that command is available. Choose it to open the dialog shown in Figure 2.21.

Figure 2.20   *You can change library icons.*

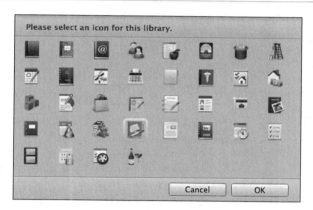

Figure 2.21   *Choose the icon for your library.*

Choose the icon that you would like for your library. Also note the preference in the following section to change the font size in the Libraries pane. The font size and your custom icons can help to organize your Libraries & Fields pane.

ⓖ *For more information on working with fields, **see** Chapter 6, "Working with Bento Fields and Calculations," p. 87.*

Setting Bento Preferences

To set Bento's preferences, you choose Bento > Preferences to open the dialog shown in Figure 2.22.

These preferences affect Bento's behavior and appearance across all libraries. If you want to change the behavior or appearance of individual libraries, Chapter 3, "Working with Bento Forms," provides that information.

ⓖ *There are three tabs at the top of Bento preferences. The first, General, is shown in Figure 2.22. The Sharing and Security tabs are discussed in Chapter 9, "Sharing Data with Other Bento Users," p. 145. On the General settings shown in Figure 2.22, the export formats are discussed in Chapter 14, "Importing and Exporting Bento Data and Libraries," p. 213.*

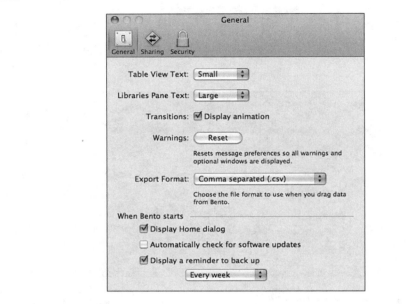

Figure 2.22 *Set Bento preferences.*

At the top of the General settings dialog, you can adjust the size of the text in the Libraries pane and the Table view. (In the Libraries pane, this adjusts the icon sizes at the same time.)

Other settings let you turn animations on and off as well as control various tasks Bento can perform at startup, such as whether or not to display the home dialog, check for software updates (you need an Internet connection for this), and remind you to backup your data.

Also useful is the Reset button. It restores Bento to its defaults so that warnings and optional windows are always displayed.

Working with Bento Forms

In this chapter you'll see how to display Bento data in forms as well as how to work with form tools and to customize forms with themes and fields.

Working with Forms

In Chapter 2, "Using the Bento Window," you saw how to use the Libraries & Fields pane to add fields. This chapter continues the discussion of fields and moves on to forms, which display the fields in a library.

> ⓖ *Forms can show fields from related libraries as you will **see** in Chapter 7, "Expanding the Inventory Library with Related Data Fields and Collections," p. 107.*

Every Bento library can be shown in a table view, which Bento generates automatically.

In Bento 3, a grid view is also generated automatically for each library. As you saw in the previous chapter, you can modify the settings for the thumbnails shown in the view.

In addition to the table and grid view, you can create and modify any number of form views. Every library must have at least one form view. In most of the templates, it is called Form, but you can change the name.

This chapter begins by exploring the Classes library template; its table view is shown in Figure 3.1. It contains a single record that is part of the template. In this chapter, you see how you can customize a copy of that form so that you have both the original and your modified form.

You select the fields to be shown in a table view by using the checkbox to the left of the field name in the Fields pane, which is at the bottom of the Libraries & Fields pane at the left of the Bento window. Because there is only one table view in a library, whether a field is displayed in that table view is an attribute of the field, and it can be set in the Fields pane.

In the navigation bar at the top of the Bento window, you can switch to the grid view as shown in Figure 3.2.

The thumbnail in the grid view has been enlarged using the zoom control in the upper right area of the grid view. As you saw in the previous chapter, it can display a reduced-size image of a form or one or more of the images in a library.

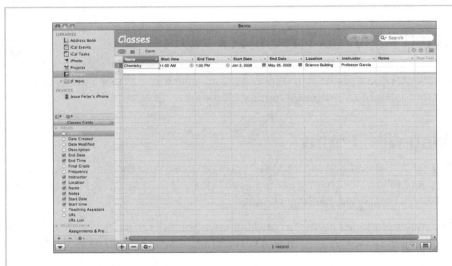

Figure 3.1   *Display the Classes template in table view.*

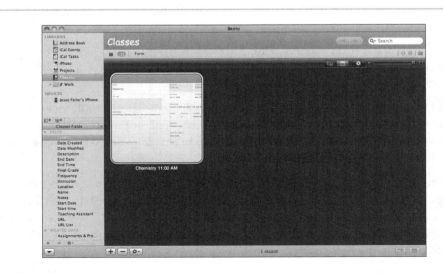

Figure 3.2   *Use the Bento grid view.*

In the navigation bar, the table and grid icons are always at the left. Moving to the right, you find a vertical dividing line and then one or more forms. In the Classes template, if you click the Form view you will see the form shown in Figure 3.3. This is a form view, and the default view is called Form in this and many templates. To be very precise, this is the Form form, but you do not have to worry about that technicality if it gives you a headache.

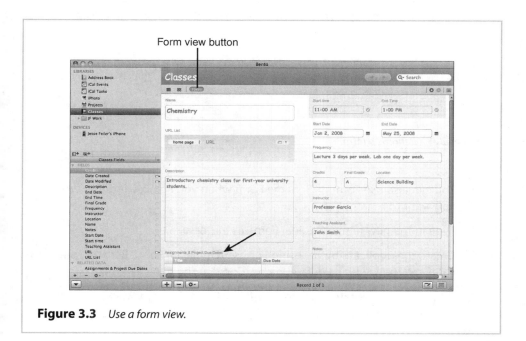

Figure 3.3 *Use a form view.*

The Fields pane makes a distinction between fields in the current library and those in related data. You can see this clearly in the Assignments & Projects Due Dates field, a field that shows related records from iCal. It shows up below the Fields section in a Related Data section, as you see in Figure 3.3.

In form view, you are able to rename a form, create new forms, and delete a form. (Except for the last one—there must always be at least one form in the library.) The form in the Classes template is called Form. For this chapter, you are modifying that form. The safest way to do that is to rename it "Original Form" and then to duplicate it and work on the duplicate.

 **LET ME TRY IT**

Duplicate and Rename a Form

Duplicating and renaming a form is a good way to safeguard your existing form before making changes.

1. Change the existing form's name so that you can revert to it if necessary. To change a form's name, double-click its name in the navigation bar to open the dialog shown in Figure 3.4. Note that as you change the Form name, these changes are immediately reflected on the navigation bar.

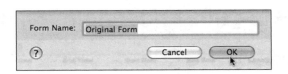

Figure 3.4   *Rename a form.*

2. You can also use Forms > Rename Form when you are viewing the form you want to rename.

3. Type in the new name: Original Form, in this case.

4. Create the duplicate by choosing Forms > Duplicate Form. Bento duplicates the form, with its default name "Copy" at the end.

5. Rename the duplicate form from "Original Form Copy" to "My Form" in the same way you renamed Form to Original Form. Now you are ready to go.

 SHOW ME   **Media 3.1—A video about how to duplicate and rename a form**
Access this video file through your registered Web Edition at my.safaribooksonline.com/9780131388611/media.

Using Form Tools

You can customize a form in three ways. *Direct manipulation* lets you resize and move fields by showing their handles and then dragging the handles or the field to its new size and location. A selected form or fields within it can also be customized using menu commands. A button in the lower right corner of the Bento window lets you show the Form tools, as you can see in Figure 3.5. You have already seen how to use the Form tool at the left: It opens the dialog shown previously in

Figure 3.4 to rename the current form. You see how to use the other tools through-out this book. Most of them provide alternate access to menu commands (for which you frequently have other access through keyboard shortcuts). Instead of the button, you can use View > Show Form Tools to show the Form tools.

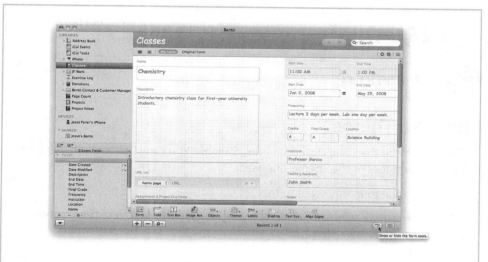

Figure 3.5   *Show the Form tools.*

 TELL ME MORE   **Media 3.2—A discussion about how, when, and why to use form tools**

Access this audio recording through your registered Web Edition at my.safaribooksonline.com/9780131388611/media.

Customizing a Form with Themes

Like Keynote with its styles, Bento lets you apply visual themes to your forms. These coordinated appearances combine a selection of colors and fonts in various styles. With a form selected, you can change its theme by choosing Forms > Theme Chooser. Unlike Keynote, Bento does not allow you to change the details of the themes. However, because of the large number of provided themes, you are likely to find themes you like.

A Bento theme is totally separate from your data. That means you can switch themes at any time without affecting your data. The various templates use a variety of themes, but you can change them at will.

If you want to be sophisticated about your Bento themes, you can select several of them to use for specific purposes, such as displaying confidential data from work, displaying social data, and the like.

Themes are applied to the active form; when you go to a table or grid view, that theme is applied to the table or grid view. If you then go to another form in the library that uses a different theme, that other theme is applied to the table or grid view when you navigate from the second form to the table view.

 **LET ME TRY IT**

Choose a Theme

There are more than two dozen themes available. You can choose them using the Themes form tool or the Theme Chooser.

1. Go to the form you want to theme.

2. To use the Theme form tool, show the Form tools and select the Themes tool as shown in Figure 3.6.

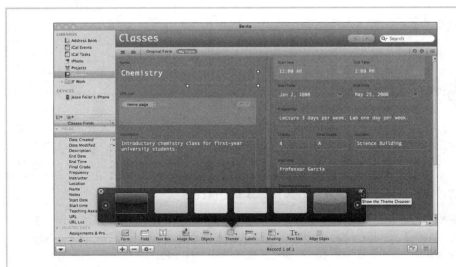

Figure 3.6   *Use the Themes form tool and Theme browser to select a theme.*

3. When you click it, you see the available themes in the small window that appears above the tools. (The downward pointing arrow in the Mac interface always means that another window will be opened rather than having a simple action performed.) You can select the theme you want to use and see it applied to your form as you watch.

4. Click the close box in the upper left corner to dismiss the themes.

5. You can also open the Theme Chooser dialog for the current form by using Forms > Theme Chooser as shown in Figure 3.7.

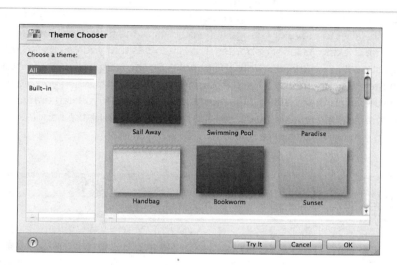

Figure 3.7 *Use Theme Chooser to vary the look of your forms.*

6. Select the theme you want to try. Click Try It to see it take effect in the window behind the Theme Chooser. You can resize the dialog somewhat so that you can see the effects while it is still open.

7. Click Choose to apply the theme and close the Theme Chooser.

8. If you do not want to change the theme, click Cancel to close the Theme Chooser with no changes.

TIP

If you are not very familiar with Bento's themes, make a note of the theme you are changing from so that you can change back to it easily without searching through all the themes to find out which one it was.

SHOW ME   Media 3.3—A video about applying a new theme to a form

Access this video file through your registered Web Edition at
my.safaribooksonline.com/9780131388611/media.

Customizing a Form's Fields

To customize a library's table view, you use the Fields pane (to control which fields are shown) and directly manipulate the table. You can reorder columns, show or hide the summary row, and change column width. You can customize a form by clicking its label to move or change it. If you click in the field itself, you are able to enter data. Clicking its label or border shows handles that you can use to resize the field, as shown in Figure 3.8. (Note the handles on the Name field; note, too that the pointer has changed to a hand from the normal pointer when you are editing fields rather than their data.) When the handles are visible, you can drag on the field's border to move it. If you click in the center of the field, the handles disappear, and you are able to enter data.

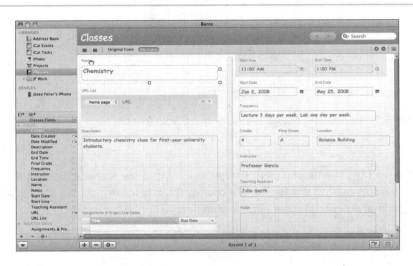

Figure 3.8   *Move and reshape fields in Bento.*

You can add fields to a form by simply dragging them from the Fields pane. Bento puts the labels in the appropriate location and coordinates their appearance with the appearance of the relevant field using the currently selected theme. When you drag a field from the Fields pane into a form that you are editing, an outline of the label and data field appears as soon as you move your mouse into the Records area, as shown in Figure 3.9. Note that a field can appear only once on a given form. It can appear on as many forms as you have, but only once on each.

Some fields require more than one data entry element; if so, they are shown in the outline and are placed in the form as soon as you release the mouse button. A heavy line shows you where in the form the new field and label are placed. In

Figure 3.9, a URL list is being placed on the form; it is one of the field types that require several elements for display and entry.

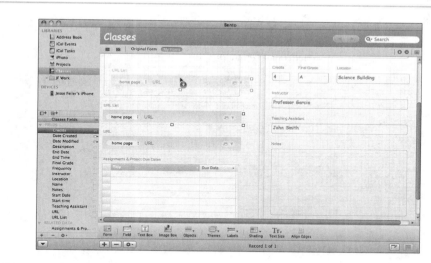

Figure 3.9 *Bento automatically provides the label and data entry fields.*

⊙ *For more details about these composite data fields, **see** Chapter 5, "Working with Phone, URL, IM, and Address Fields and Lists in Contacts," p. 77.*

After a field and its label have been placed on a form, you can change its width or height by selecting it and dragging the right or bottom border. You can also rearrange fields; just drag them up or down or from column to column. Bento takes care of everything for you—fields move aside as needed. And, of course, the tab order remains logical (top to bottom and left to right in column one, and then on to column two with the same ordering). To rearrange fields after you have already added them, you click the label or border of a field to begin editing it.

Bento provides you with several formatting objects that you can add to a form using the Objects form tool pop-up menu. Figure 3.10 shows how you can add a *horizontal separator*—it is being placed just below the Description field.

A horizontal separator is visible in the finished form. Two other formatting objects are not visible except when you are editing the form. In Figure 3.11, you can see a column separator between the two columns. Although it is not visible after you have finished editing the form, it helps Bento keep the columns in line.

You can also add a *spacer*. As you can see, Bento positions fields in each column of a form starting at the left of each row. If you want to indent a field, add a spacer at the beginning of the row. It will not be visible, but it will have the effect of pushing the fields in that row to the right. You can resize the spacer so that the fields look exactly the way you want them to. You can see a spacer placed in Figure 3.11. It pushes the field and label to the right (both field and label automatically move together).

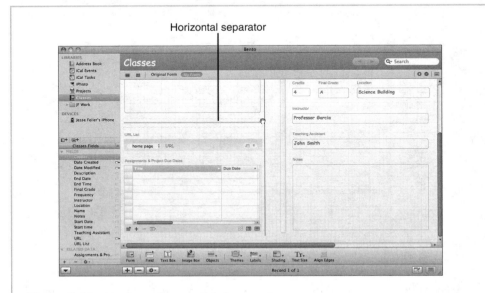

Figure 3.10   *Use form objects to help format a form.*

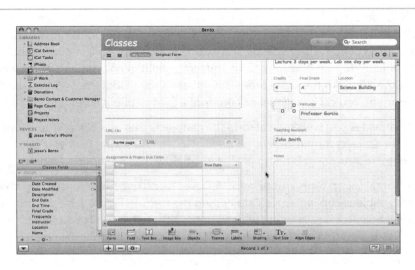

Figure 3.11   *Only the horizontal rule is directly visible in the finished form.*

Add these objects by using the Objects button in the Form tools or by using the appropriate commands in the Insert menu.

Table 3.1 describes each of the form tools from left to right and provides keyboard equivalents.

> **NOTE**
>
> Figures illustrating the use of the various tools are referenced in Table 3.1. Some of them are covered in later chapters.

Table 3.1   Form Tools

Tool	Equivalent	Purpose
Form	Double-click form name in the navigation bar or Forms > Rename Form.	Change a form's name (Figure 3.4)
Field	Opens the Create a Field dialog	Open the Create a Field dialog (Figure 6.2).
Text Box	Insert > Text Box	You can type anything you want in the text box, and you can move it around the form just like a field. Unlike a field, this is not data from your library; it is simply text that appears on the form.
Image Box	Insert > Image Box	Creates an image box. See Chapter 6.
Objects	Insert > Horizontal Separator Insert > Column Divider Insert > Spacer	A spacer is a blank area that also can be moved around. You use it to add space between fields. There is also a horizontal separator (a line) that can be used to separate groups of fields.
Themes	Forms > Choose Theme	Select a theme.
Labels	Forms > Labels	Choose Above or Beside as well as Small, Medium or Large.
Shading	Forms > Shading	Choose None, Light, or Dark for selected field(s).
Text Size	Forms > Text Size	Choose Smallest to Largest for selected field(s).
Align Edges	Forms > Align Right Edges	Align right edges of selected Align Right Edges objects. Other edges remain where they were. Note that this command is not available if the right edges are already aligned.

TIP

Be wary of going overboard with these design elements. If you find yourself needing to organize your forms with spacers and separators, maybe you would be better off splitting your form into two separate forms. As described in Chapter 7, "Expanding the Inventory Library with Related Records and Collections," you can use collections and related records to bring whole sets of data onto a form in a simple way. Bento works best for most people when you can see all the data elements in a form without scrolling the window.

The field consists of the label and the data entry section(s); a background may be shaded for the entire rectangle that contains these elements. In the Format menu or the Form tools, you can choose the degree of shading you want. They can be effective in highlighting essential (or nonessential) information as long as you use shading consistently.

You can also change the size of the text in the data fields, as well as the size of the label. Finally, you can select two or more fields and align their right edges. You do this by expanding the narrower fields' widths so that all are consistent.

 **LET ME TRY IT**

Copy Forms within a Library

If you have a library with one or more collections within it, you can copy your forms to and from the library and each of its collections so that your design work can be reused. It also makes it easier to use the library and its collections if the forms are the same in each environment.

1. Start from a library that contains one or more collections or from a collection (it is always part of a library).

2. Navigate to the form you want to copy.

3. Control-click the form name in the navigation bar to bring up the shortcuts menu as shown in Figure 3.12.

4. Select where you want to copy the form to. Your choices will be the library itself and all of its collections except for the environment you are currently in.

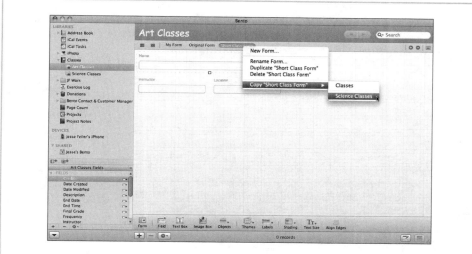

Figure 3.12   *Copy a form with the shortcuts menu.*

 SHOW ME   **Media 3.4—A video about copying a form within a library**

Access this video file through your registered Web Edition at
my.safaribooksonline.com/9780131388611/media.

Building a Bento Library from Your Own Data

This chapter shows you how to organize your data and how to import data from other sources such as spreadsheets.

Getting Started Organizing Your Data

In the first few chapters of this book, you saw the basics of Bento: how to use the Bento window, how to create and delete records, and how to use the Bento data management tools such as finding and sorting. You even saw how to create databases from the Bento templates and started finding out how you can customize the look and feel of your personal databases.

This chapter helps you move in a new direction. You know the Bento basics; now what can you actually—practically—use it for in your own life? The acid test is whether Bento can help you organize all the data you have floating around your computer. Many people have accumulated lots of data over the years, and computer disks have grown bigger and bigger. If you buy a new computer periodically, the hard disk will be larger than the one you are used to, and you might be able to move all your data from the old crowded computer and its hard disk to the new hard disk and have plenty of space left over.

The data can consist of old emails and documents that just might be needed some day, which can be in the form of spreadsheets and even a variety of database formats, large and small. Maybe you have AppleWorks files that you rely on for your daily activities. The format may be old, but the data is valuable, and—most important—Bento allows you to get to it.

This chapter shows you how to go about moving data into Bento, where it can be stored and searched quickly. If you are using old software to manage your data, you may legitimately be worried that at some point the software might break and you may not be able to find a new version, leaving your data inaccessible. (The term for such data and software is *legacy*, as in legacy software or legacy data.) Although you probably do not want to think about it, the fact is that data stored in

old software and unsupported formats is a critical risk to any person or organization that relies on it.

 Ⓖ *Importing data into a new library as described in this chapter is simpler than
importing data into an existing library. For more details on importing and exporting
data and libraries, **see** Chapter 14, "Importing and Exporting Bento Data and
Libraries," p. 213.*

Reviewing Your Legacy Data

Moving data into Bento is not difficult, and it is something that you should do for
your legacy data. Start by protecting your most important data and the data for
which your applications are old and not easily replaced or updated. Often, the easiest way to do this is to move them into Bento.

Data that you move into Bento is going to wind up as a set of records with fields in
them because that is the basic Bento paradigm. Often, you move data from spreadsheets or database tables because those are comparable structures. Sometimes,
the data is in word processing documents formatted as a table. Free-format data
that is not tabular in nature is not a particularly good candidate for Bento import.

NOTE

Importing is used to describe the process of reading a file and converting it into
one or more Bento records automatically. Though importing data that is in tabular format can be a simple, automated process, even the most free-format data
can still be moved into Bento by copying and pasting each data element indi-
vidually into a Bento record.

Working with Data Formats

Instead of converting your data into records and fields, you can often take the
existing file and reference it from Bento. (Referencing a file means just that: the file
remains where it is and Bento can reference it to provide access to its data.) You
can import references to files in Bento, so your movies, free-form poetry, and other
data are accessible and organized by Bento. However, remember that the application that Bento uses to open the file needs to be available. Storing a reference to a
file that needs to be opened by a program you do not have or that is no longer
available does not do you any good.

Fortunately, many programs allow you to save your documents in alternate formats. These are generally available in Save As or Export commands located in the File menu. Figure 4.1 shows the Microsoft Word Save As menu.

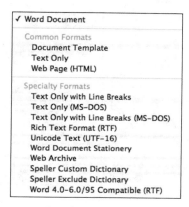

Figure 4.1   *Many applications let you save a copy of a file in a new format.*

These formats are a combination of proprietary formats and formats that are widely available. Many programs support older versions of their native formats for reading and writing. Word, for example, lets you save backward-compatible files going back to Word 4.0. You can also save the basic text in a variety of formats; these files can be opened by any program that can read text. Rich Text Format (RTF) is a standard format that preserves a great deal of style information including fonts and basic paragraph formatting. Saving old word-processing files in RTF or a text-based format makes them accessible by many programs.

The iWork applications Pages and Numbers use an Export command, as shown in Figure 4.2. In iWork, the Save As command is used to save a copy of the file with another name and to control options such as whether movies are saved in the file. These are still Pages and Numbers files; Export is reserved for changing the file format. Also note in Figure 4.2 that you can set security for the exported files. If you are working on your own computer, you can use the defaults, which have no security settings. If you are using a shared computer, consider using security depending on the circumstances of the data and the user environment.

Notice that you can save Numbers files as native Excel spreadsheets, and you can save Pages files as native Word documents. Plain text and RTF are also supported in Pages, while comma-separated value (CSV) is supported in Numbers. Both support Portable Document Format (PDF).

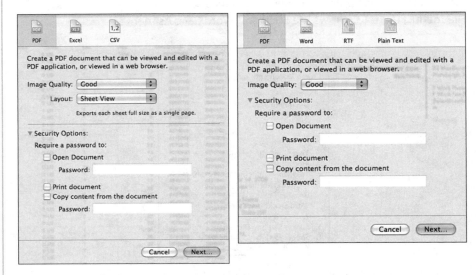

Figure 4.2   *iWork applications use the Export command.*

A standard installation of Mac OS X includes TextEdit, which can read and write both plain text and RTF files. This means that if you convert old files to either of those formats, you are able to store references to them in Bento and open them automatically. (You can also open them from the Finder.)

If you do not have Adobe Reader to read PDF files, you can download it for free from www.adobe.com. This provides you with another standard format to use to convert your legacy files. It also provides you with a safety net in case your legacy application does not support Save As or Export. In the Print dialog that is used by most applications, you can use the PDF button in the lower left to save the printed output as a PDF file, as shown in Figure 4.3.

In most cases, this means that if you can print it, you can save the image as a PDF file and open that with a double-click that launches Adobe Reader if necessary. (Many applications, including Safari, can open PDF files themselves.)

If you are worried about not being able to open old files in the future, converting them to text, RTF, or PDF should solve the problem.

A related issue of file formats arises with media files. You can use Bento's media fields to store images, sounds, and movies. Supported file types include PDF, JPG, TIFF, GIF, MP3, PICT, MOV, and PSD (Photoshop).

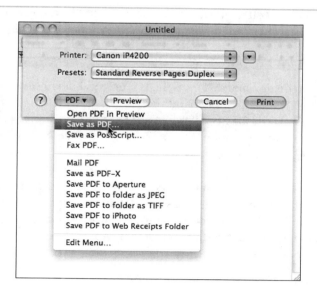

Figure 4.3 *Save printouts as PDF files.*

In Bento 3, integration with iPhoto makes your photo libraries easily available to Bento. There is more on this in Chapter 10, "Using Built-In Bento Libraries for Address Book and iPhoto," p. 155.

If you have an image, sound, or movie that is not in a supported format, you can often use the Export or Save As command in the other application to convert it.

SHOW ME   Media 4.1—A video about using file references in Bento
Access this video file through your registered Web Edition at
my.safaribooksonline.com/9780131388611/media.

Performing a Basic Data Import

This section walks you through the process of importing data either from your own data (current or legacy) or data that you download from the Web. CSV is generally provided as an exportable format from spreadsheets such as Excel or Numbers and databases such as FileMaker Pro.

The data used in this example is from the U.S. Census Bureau; it consists of population projections from 2004 to 2030, as well as the 2000 census data. The data is arranged by state, age, and sex. It consists of 13,572 records, so it provides a good example of a fairly substantial data import. In addition, the data demonstrates some of the issues you need to watch out for when importing data.

> **NOTE**
> The data file can be downloaded from the U.S. Census Bureau website (www.census.gov) along with a number of other data files. In addition, you can download a ZIP archive of the file from this book's site as described in the introduction. Despite the massive amount of data in the file, the file itself is actually quite small, just 2.3MB; the ZIP archive is 1MB.

Bento supports a variety of input formats. Comma-separated values (CSV), is a common format for spreadsheets and some databases. In addition to CSV data, you can import data directly from Excel spreadsheets, from Numbers spreadsheets, and from tab-delimited files such as those created by AppleWorks. The basic process is the same as importing CSV data.

CSV data can be numeric or text and looks like this:

```
red, blue, green
1, 2, 3
hello there, Henry IV, 20,354
```

As you can see, the commas separate the data values, although in other formats you may see a different separator such as a semi-colon used. The first thing to check in your data is whether it contains commas that are not separators. For example, in the third line of this example, are there three values (the last one being a number—20,354), or are there four values (the last two being two numbers—20 and 354)?

If data contains embedded commas, you can place the entire value inside quotation marks. There is no ambiguity in this line of data, which contains three (not four) values:

```
Hello there, Henry IV, "20,354"
```

If the data itself contains quotation marks, double them. For example, the first element of this line of data might be a quote that is written:

```
"Hello, there"
```

If you want to preserve the quotes, it should be written as:

```
""Hello, there""
```

In most cases, you do not have to worry about this problem. If you are working with an application that can export CSV data (such as FileMaker Pro, Numbers, or Excel), all this is done for you automatically.

The issues of embedded commas and quotes are one of the reasons some people prefer tab-delimited formats. With these, each value is separated from the next one on a line by a tab character. This means that you can easily use commas and quotation marks within the data. However, the problem is not solved if your data itself contains tab characters. Furthermore, if you are manually checking the data, commas or semi-colons are easy to spot: tab characters do not print. Fortunately, for any given set of data, it is usually possible to pick a delimited format that is satisfactory, at least for most of the data. The message to be learned is that relying on any characters to delimit data fields is prone to problems. Get the data into a format where this is not an issue: Bento's internal format is one such, as are the formats used internally by Excel and Numbers. When Bento reads such a file, it can correctly read commas, semi-colons, and tabs without confusion. And once your data is stored in a format that is unambiguous about its delimiters, you are safe.

Another thing Bento handles for you automatically is labeling the data. If you have labels in your file, the first record consists of the names of the fields being exported. (This may be an export option in the program from which you are exporting data.) If this option is available, use it; it makes your import easier, as you see later in this section.

 TELL ME MORE   Media 4.2—A discussion about checking your data conversion
Access this audio recording through your registered Web Edition at my.safaribooksonline.com/9780131388611/media.

 **LET ME TRY IT**

Import Data Into a New Bento Library

The simplest way to import data into Bento is to automatically create a new library.

1. Begin by choosing File > Import. The Import window shown in Figure 4.4 opens.

2. Select the file to import, and, for its destination, select New Library. Provide a name for the library. Bento attempts to open the file and display the first record in the main section of the Import window. In this case, the first record contains field names, and they are displayed. Use the left and right arrows below the data display to move through the file. As you can see from the checkbox beneath the field values, you have an option of whether or not to use the first record as field names.

TIP

As shown at the bottom of Figure 4.4, you can step through the data and choose any record to use as the column names. That record is treated as the first record in the file, and the remaining records are imported. If you select record 5 as the column names, the data import starts with column 6.

3. As you can see, you can use a pop-up menu in Figure 4.4 to choose the delimiter for your data. If you are uncertain which character to use, experiment with the three choices. When you hit on the correct one, the display at the bottom of Figure 4.4 will look better organized than with the other choices.

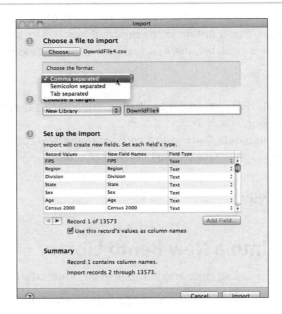

Figure 4.4   *Begin to import data.*

4. Step through a few records, as shown in Figure 4.5, to make certain that the data looks correct. Note that the field names picked up from the first (or selected) record in Figure 4.4 are shown next to the data values as you step through each record. If commas or quotation marks are mismatched, you will often see the problem here, and you can correct the import data. Also check the total number of records. If it is off, that, too, is likely a comma or quotation mark issue.

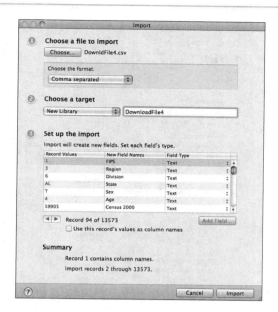

Figure 4.5   *Step through the records.*

5. By default, all fields are imported as text. Change the field types to the actual types of the data. Do this based on the field names as well as on the data. For example, data that is organized into tabular form often contains totals and subtotals. These can pose issues that you need to deal with. In the population data, for example, you can easily see that the Age field contains the age of people. However, that does not mean that it is a numeric field.

    The Age field sometimes contains the word "Total," as shown in Figure 4.5. In addition, it contains the value 85+ for people 85 or older.

    Figure 4.6 shows how you can change the field types. You can also indicate that a field is not to be imported. Remember that the field names and types apply to all records. Changing them in the Import dialog has to be done once—not separately—for each imported record.

6. Now you are ready to import the data. Bento is very fast. (This data import takes less than a minute.) Bento creates a library for you, and you can then use the techniques in the preceding chapters to rearrange the fields and customize it, as shown in Figure 4.7.

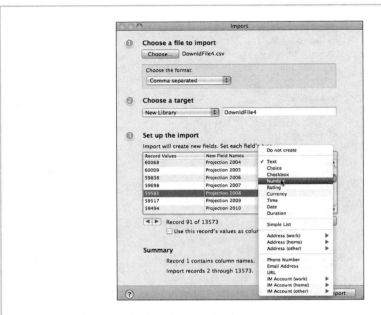

Figure 4.6   *Change field types as needed.*

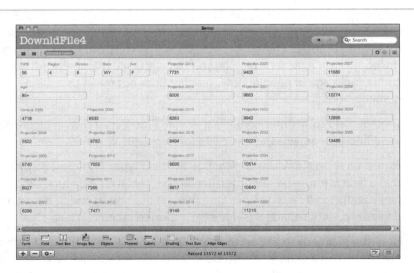

Figure 4.7   *Customize the library.*

7. Here is another area where you can check the data import. You can show the
summary row in table view and total various columns or count the values as
shown in Figure 4.8.

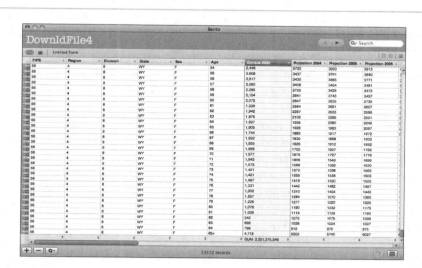

Figure 4.8   *Use the summary row to check your data import.*

Ⓖ *You will find more about using the summary row in Chapter 6, "Working with
Bento Fields and Calculations," p. 87.*

You can do this in conjunction with finding subsets of data. This is one of the reasons you need to know what you are importing. This data set (like many) includes
total and subtotal rows. That means that the totals of columns are much too high
because they contain basic data as well as totals and subtotals. This is a common
occurrence. You may want to use what are called *check totals*, which are simple
arithmetic totals of the numbers in a column, possibly including subtotals and
totals. The number is meaningless except to check that the values have been
entered or transferred correctly.

In fact, there are quite a few anomalies that you may run into. The next section
gives you some tips about cleaning up data.

 SHOW ME   **Media 4.3—A video about importing data into a new
Bento library**
*Access this video file through your registered Web Edition at
my.safaribooksonline.com/9780131388611/media.*

Cleaning Up Imported Data

When you are importing data to Bento or any other destination, you often need to do some cleanup work. It is usually easiest to do the cleanup before the import. This is because if you are using the original program, you have all the tools available to manipulate the data. In addition, the cleaner the data, the fewer import errors you have.

The most basic form of cleanup is to verify the data. Are the phone numbers still valid? Are the names correctly spelled? Of course, while it is desirable to clean up the data as much as possible and as early as possible in the process, this is the real world. One way to handle data importing is to add a new field to the Bento library after you have imported the data. Make it a checkbox field called Verified. Leave the data in its basic state, and, as you use it in Bento, check that it is valid. This means that the data you actually use is cleaned up before the rarely used data. Check the Verified checkbox so that you know you have checked individual data records. Gradually, you will clean up most or even all your data. (And remember that you can find data that is not verified using Advanced Find.)

TIP

A variation on this strategy works for data that can change over time. Instead of a Verified checkbox, create a date field called Last Checked. Whenever you check the data (perhaps by actually using the email address or telephone number), choose Insert > Current Date and Time to update that field.

There is another common cleanup process that's often necessary when importing spreadsheets. Spreadsheets today occupy a place somewhere in the middle of databases (because they support data storage and searching), word processing documents (because you can format them for display and printing), and traditional data tables (rows and columns). The hardest spreadsheets to import are those that are specially formatted to look their best. As you have seen, Bento is happy to import an initial record with field names. But what happens when you have five beautifully formatted rows of text with titles centered (and perhaps with parenthetical comments)?

What happens is that you have to remove all that beautiful formatting and extraneous text so that you have only a single title row (or none at all). Naturally, you should do this in a copy of the original spreadsheet. (To help solve this problem, use the option to select a row other than the literal first row of the table for column names and a location to start importing.)

In the old days, a spreadsheet document consisted of a single sheet. Today, a spreadsheet can have several sheets within it, and formulas can reference all the sheets within a spreadsheet workbook. But old habits die hard, and many spreadsheets have a single set of rows and columns in the upper left and a variety of smaller rows and columns tables (each with its own nicely formatted labels and titles) all over the spreadsheet. The only way to successfully import this data is to split the complex spreadsheet apart into basic rows and columns tables, each with at most a single title row at the top. Or in Bento simply copy these smaller tables and paste them into a table view.

NOTE

Dealing with these spreadsheets is not really a Bento issue. If you have one of these old spreadsheets, it still functions better as a spreadsheet if you split it apart into separate sheets, each of which is a simple rows and columns table.

Finally, consider cleaning up spreadsheets by removing total and subtotal rows. You can use these values for checking your import, but by stripping the spreadsheet down to its data and removing calculated totals and pretty formatting, you will make your life easier in the long run. (You can also omit them from the import dialog rather than deleting them from the spreadsheet itself.)

 SHOW ME   Media 4.4—A video about cleaning up a spreadsheet to import

Access this video file through your registered Web Edition at
my.safaribooksonline.com/9780131388611/media.

5

Working with Phone, URL, IM, and Address Fields and Lists in Contacts

This chapter shows you how to use the Contacts library and how to enter data in address, email, and URL lists.

Exploring the Contacts Library

One of the libraries that comes with Bento is the Contacts library. It lets you store contact information such as names, addresses (physical, email, and instant messaging, or IM), birthdays, and job information. As shipped, it provides a powerful personal contacts database, and as you see in this chapter, much of its functionality is provided by standard Bento data and interface elements that you can easily use in other contexts.

Bento, of course, also ships with a library that is integrated with your Mac OS X Address Book application. The Bento Address Book library has even more information than does the Contacts library. Furthermore, it has the enormously important feature of automatically being integrated and synchronized with your Address Book data as necessary. This synchronization can extend far beyond your computer so that your Address Book data can automatically be synchronized with your MobileMe account, with your other Macs, and with your iPhone, PDA, or other synchronizable device. In fact, by using MobileMe, this synchronization can extend to PCs running Windows.

⏎ *You find more on these matters in Chapter 10, "Using Built-In Bento Libraries for Address Book and iPhoto," p. 155.*

Starting by exploring the nonintegrated and synchronized Contacts library lets you look at a simple case of real-life Bento use, including cases where the lack of integration and synchronization has its advantages. The most obvious such cases are those in which you need to keep track of contacts that you do not want to mingle with your own contacts. If you are coaching a sports team, managing the membership of an association, or working on a political campaign, it can be important that the data for the team, association, or campaign be kept separate from your own personal data. Furthermore, in some cases, your role as guardian of the contact data may be temporary—perhaps just for the year. Thus, you need a powerful way to organize the data, you need a tool that lets you quickly import last year's data from the person who managed it in the past, and you also need a tool that lets you easily export it in a commonly used format so that next year's data guardian can import it into whatever software on whatever computer will be used in the future. You can use groups in Address Book to organize your contacts, but if you really need separation, nothing beats a completely separate library.

○ *For more details on importing and exporting data and libraries, **see** Chapter 14, "Importing and Exporting Bento Data and Libraries," p. 213.*

Start your exploration by creating a Contacts library in Bento. Choose File > New Library From Template or click the + button beneath the libraries list at the top of the Libraries & Fields pane. This opens the New Library dialog, as shown in Figure 5.1.

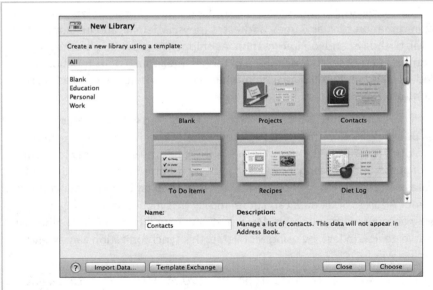

Figure 5.1   *Create a new Bento Contacts library.*

The Bento library templates are organized into groups (Education, Personal, and Work); some, including the Contacts library, are available from each of the groups.

TIP

In the New Library dialog, libraries with the same name are, indeed, the same libraries no matter which groups they appear in. If they are customized for use in a specific context, they are renamed.

As you explore this dialog, remember that the lower right of the dialog gives you information about each library as you click it. Also, you can rename the library you are about to create by typing the new name at the lower left corner of the dialog. Particularly if your Contacts library is to be for a special purpose, consider naming it appropriately right from the start.

When you click the Choose button (shown in the lower left of Figure 5.1), Bento creates the new library. As always with a Bento template, a record with sample data is created, as shown in Figure 5.2.

Figure 5.2   *Click Choose to create the library.*

When you create a library, you have at least three views of the library available from the navigation bar at the top of the Records area: a table view and a grid view (both of these are automatically created by Bento) as well as at least one form view. In the case of the Contacts library, there are two form views. The first one is Overview, shown in Figure 5.2; the second is Details, shown in Figure 5.3.

Bento implements a *split view* as shown in Figure 5.4. This shows a multi-record view (either table view or grid view) at the top and a form view of a single record at the bottom. You can switch from table to grid view and back while the split view is open, and you can switch from one form to another as well. You can drag the divider up or down to resize the two views. Enter or exit the split view with View > Split View or the button at the right of the bottom row of the navigation bar.

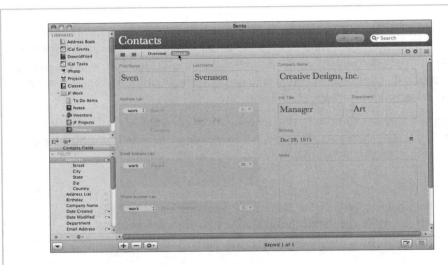

Figure 5.3   *Details form of the Contacts library.*

Figure 5.4   *The Bento split view displays multiple records in a table or grid view at the same time as a single record in a form view.*

Working with Fields

The heart of the Contacts library are the address fields and lists for addresses, phone numbers, IM addresses, and email addresses. Bento manages these special-purpose fields and lists for you. In this section, you see how to use them, and in the following section, you see how easily you can create them.

To enter data in any field, just click it to highlight it as the current field, as shown in Figure 5.5. Some new data has been added for existing fields in this way: in Figure 5.5 you see an address, a phone number, an email address, and a URL.

Figure 5.5 *Enter data.*

At the left of the Details form for Contacts, you find lists for addresses, email addresses, phone numbers, and URLs (note the field names above the fields). Although the sample data has only one item in each list, you can easily create new items, as you see in the following section.

 **LET ME TRY IT**

Enter Contact Data

The best way to explore the Contacts library and its features is to work with it. Create a new record, and then fill in its data. Experiment with your own data: do not make up data because the email and mapping links will not work properly.

1. If you haven't already, create a new Contacts library using File > New Library From Template or the + beneath the Libraries pane.

2. Click Overview to go to the Overview form.

3. Create a new record with + beneath the form view or Records > New Record.

4. Enter the first name.

5. Either click in the last name field or tab to it and enter the last name.

6. Click or tab again to enter the address. Click or tab to continue entering the city, state, zip code, and country.

7. Continue in the same way to enter the email address. Click the button to the right of the email address to open a pre-addressed email message in a new window.

 SHOW ME   Media 5.1—A video about entering contact data
Access this video file through your registered Web Edition at
my.safaribooksonline.com/9780131388611/media.

Working with Address, Email, Phone Number, and URL Lists

There are always two buttons at the right side of each item in a list field. The first does something specific to that type of list field — for example, for an address, the first button opens a map; for an email address, it creates a new Mail message to that address. The second opens a contextual menu of commands that can be applied to the specific element of the list. Figure 5.6 shows the menu for an address item.

The layout of those menus is always the same:

- The first item is the default action that is also accessible from the left-hand button.

- The last two items add another element to the list or delete the current one.

- Other actions may appear in between.

The default actions for the list elements are:

- Map an address

- Send an email

- Display a phone number in large type

- Open the IM account in iChat

- Open a URL, which lets you both open and edit a URL

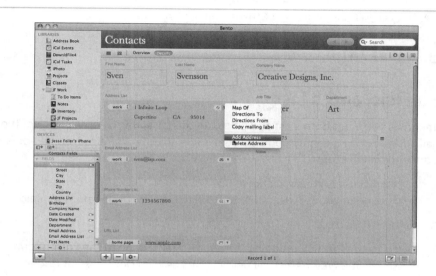

Figure 5.6   *Use shortcuts for elements in a list.*

The address field has additional actions. They are:

- Map Of

- Directions To

- Directions From

- Copy Mailing Label (This combines the address elements into a single block of text that you can paste onto an envelope with proper spacing and line breaks)

NOTE

The mapping and directions actions open Google Maps and fill in the appropriate address automatically.

Adding Address Fields and Lists to Your Forms

If a field is defined as being one of the address types (address, phone number, email address, URL, or IM account), the Fields pane in the Bento window shows the field as well as a list for that address type. You can add either or both to your form simply by dragging it (or them) to the Records area.

 **LET ME TRY IT**

Use a Field and a List

Sometimes you want both a list and a field. In this case, the list contains all of the email addresses for a contact; one of them is identified as Preferred, and it appears prominently on the form.

1. In your Contacts library, create a new email field. Click the + beneath the fields pane or choose Insert > New Field to create a phone number field.

2. Name it Preferred.

3. Add it to the form by dragging it from the Fields pane to the Form. Figure 5.7 shows the Preferred email field (as well as a Do Not Give Out phone field) added to the form.

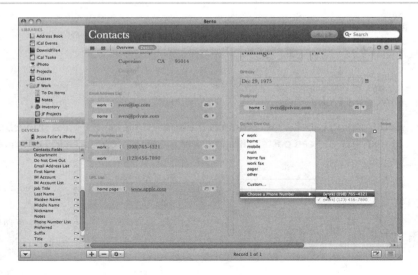

Figure 5.7   *As opposed to lists, fields let you see a single address at a time.*

4. Enter an email address. You will immediately see it shown in a new line in the Email list.

5. You can repeat the same process with a Do Not Call phone number field.

6. When you have a field created, you can use the second button to the right of an entry in a phone number, email, or URL list to change that field's value to one of the other items in the list as you see in Figure 5.7.

 SHOW ME   Media 5.2—A video about using a field and a list
Access this video file through your registered Web Edition at
my.safaribooksonline.com/9780131388611/media.

A given address type has only one list. Thus, if you have a URL field called MyURL and another URL field called YourURL, there is a single URL list that contains all the values from both MyURL and YourURL.

As you can see in Figure 5.7, you can use the combination of lists and an individual address to indicate some special value such as a phone number that is not to be given out. You can create labels for phone numbers and other addresses, but sometimes you need a combination of categories such as shown here: a home phone that also must not be given out.

With these basic interface building blocks, Bento immediately solves a number of issues that you may have encountered in trying to customize other databases or organizers. Now that the complexities and variations of addresses are off your mind, you can explore how Bento helps you with calculating data. That is the topic of the next chapter.

 **LET ME TRY IT**

Use Contact Data

Use the data you have already entered to explore the buttons in the lists.

1. Click in the address field.

2. Add a new address by clicking the second button to the right of the address and choosing Add Address as shown previously in Figure 5.6

3. Map the address in a new window by clicking the first button to the right of the address.

4. Using the email address you have entered, create a new email message addressed to it with either of the buttons to the right of the email address.

SHOW ME   Media 5.3—A video about editing contact data
Access this video file through your registered Web Edition at
my.safaribooksonline.com/9780131388611/media.

TELL ME MORE   Media 5.4—A discussion about time-shifting your
work by using Bento Buttons
Access this audio recording through your registered Web Edition at
my.safaribooksonline.com/9780131388611/media.

Working with Bento Fields and Calculations

This chapter shows you how to create and format Bento fields.

Adding Calculation Fields to the Exercise Log

In the process of learning how to create forms, how to import data from a non-Bento file to a new library, and how to work with the built-in Phone, URL, IM, and Address fields and lists, you have seen the basics of using fields.

This chapter covers most of the Bento field types in detail, showing how a number of them can be used in Exercise Log and providing information about others as well (note that some Bento field types are described in other chapters).

⊕ *Phone, URL, IM, and Address fields together with their associated lists are discussed in Chapter 5, "Working with Phone, URL, IM, and Address Fields and Lists in Contacts," p. 77.*

⊕ *Media fields are discussed in Chapter 7, "Expanding the Inventory Library with Related Data Fields and Collections," p. 107 in the section, "Exploring the Inventory Library."*

⊕ *Related records list fields are discussed in Chapter 7, "Expanding the Inventory Library with Related Data Fields and Collections," p. 107.*

⊕ *Message list fields are discussed in Chapter 12, "Working with Bento's Projects Library to Use Related Records from iCal Tasks, iCal Events, Apple Mail, and Address Book," p. 183 in the section, "Working with Related Records from Mail."*

⊕ *File list fields are discussed in Chapter 13, "Designing a Projects Library to Share on Your LAN and Synchronize with Your iPhone," p. 195.*

Exercise Log is one of the built-in Bento libraries. You can see the basic library in Figure 6.1.

This library provides a simple way to track your exercise routine. You can expand it with some new fields that make it a bit more useful (and that demonstrate features of Bento fields in the process).

Figure 6.1   *Explore the Exercise Log library.*

In the basic library, you enter all the data, including the calories burned and the duration of the exercise. With a little effort, you can modify it so that calories burned and duration are both calculated.

To do this calculation, you need to add two fields:

- A stop time field so that you can calculate the duration.

- Number of calories burned for a given unit of time for the exercise that you are doing. Given that number, you can then multiply it by the calculated duration to compute the number of calories burned. This field can be called calorie rate.

There is a simple reason why these changes can improve the library (other than providing an example of how to use fields and calculations). Calculating the duration from a start and stop time is a simple calculation, and it is one that occasionally trips people up when they do it manually. With Bento, you can enter a time by clicking the clock next to a time field or by clicking the calendar next to a date field. (You see the difference later in this chapter.) By default, the current date and time are entered, and there is little room for error. Of course, that means you need access to Bento when you start and stop your exercise; without such immediate access, you can still click the clock or calendar and easily make the adjustment for the current start or stop time.

When it comes to calculating the calories burned, that, too, is not a particularly onerous task if you do it by hand. However, if you can do everything automatically after the start and stop times are entered, the margin for error is greatly reduced. (Often these simple steps generate careless errors.)

And as if that were not enough, if the calories burned per unit of time is entered into a field on the form, that value is constant for each record that uses the same type of exercise. You can just duplicate the record and change the start and stop times to have everything properly updated.

To complete the process, in addition to adding the stop time and calorie rate, you need to make the duration and calories burned fields into calculations. To do this, you can create new calculation fields and remove the old entry fields.

Creating and Formatting Date Fields in Exercise Log

In Chapter 1, "Bento: The Database for the Rest of Us," you saw the variety of fields that you can create in Bento; in Chapter 3, "Working with Bento Forms," you saw how to change the look of a library. In this section, you find a step-by-step walk-through of both processes as you create the two new fields for the stop time and calories burned per hour (calorie rate).

Creating a Stop Date Field

The Exercise Log library has a time field for you to enter the time you start the exercise. That makes sense: Time fields are for time values. But frequently if you are entering times that will delineate a period of time (rather than a specific time such as an appointment), you may not want to use the time field. Rather, you can use a date field that has the option of including month, day, year, as well as time. This makes the calculation of a duration unambiguous even if the period of time spans one or more days. Although it is unlikely that you will be running for more than a day, it is quite possible that you might be exercising at night, possibly across the midnight break from one day to another. By using a date field, you do not have to worry. (If your exercise happens to take you over the International Date Line, you will be on your own regardless of what field type you use.)

Create a Stop field by clicking the + at the bottom of the Fields pane or by choosing Insert > New Field. The dialog shown in Figure 6.2 opens.

This dialog lets you choose any of the field types you want. The buttons at the lower right let you create such a field and continue to create another field, close the dialog without saving anything, or create the single field and close the dialog so you can continue with what you were doing.

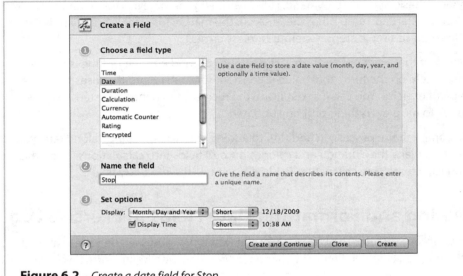

Figure 6.2   *Create a date field for Stop.*

The scrolling list of fields is divided into three groups. The first consists of basic fields such as text and numbers along with some specialized fields such as choices, checkboxes, and related data. The second set of fields includes calculations, dates and times, currency, and the like (it is shown in Figure 6.2). Except for the encrypted field, these are all discussed in this chapter. The final group consists of the address fields discussed in the previous chapter.

Date fields let you set various display options, as shown in Figure 6.2. You can choose from Month, Day, and Year or just Month and Day. You can also choose the level of detail. As you change these options, the sample data shown in Figure 6.2 changes. The detail options for dates when Month, Day, and Year are displayed are

- Short: 10/25/2008
- Medium: Oct 25, 2008
- Long: October 25, 2008
- Full: Saturday, October 25, 2008

The sequence of Month, Day, and Year is determined by your International settings in System Preferences—specifically the Formats pane.

For times, there are only two formatting choices: Short contains hours and minutes, and Medium adds seconds to the display.

For the Exercise Log, make certain that you set the options at the bottom of the dialog so that both the date and time are visible.

Now, drag the Stop field from the Fields list into the library.

Creating a Start Date Field

If you are following this procedure, you need to do the same to create a new Start field that is a date, not a time field. To do this, you first need to select the existing Start field and delete it. Then create a new Start field that is a date just as you did with the Stop field. Because it is the same as the Stop field, you can also select the Stop field in the Fields list, duplicate it, and then change the name from the default Stop 1 to Start.

 **LET ME TRY IT**

Delete, Duplicate, and Rename a Field

The process of deleting a field and then duplicating and renaming another field to replace it is very useful—and very easy in Bento.

1. Select the field you want to delete in the Fields pane (in this case, Start). Click the — below the Fields pane to delete. You will be warned that you must confirm the field deletion so that you cannot accidentally delete it.

2. Select the field you want to duplicate and rename. In this case it is the Stop field that you just created.

3. Use Edit > Duplicate Field or the Additional Commands (gear wheel) beneath the Fields pane.

4. The duplicated field has the same name as the original with a number after it. (Stop becomes Stop 1; if you duplicate it again it becomes Stop 1 1.)

5. Click the duplicated field in the Fields pane and change its name. In this case, change Stop 1 to Start.

6. The duplicated and renamed field has all the characteristics of the original field.

SHOW ME   Media 6.1—A video about deleting, duplicating, and renaming a field

Access this video file through your registered Web Edition at my.safaribooksonline.com/9780131388611/media.

With a field selected in the Fields pane, you can use the shortcuts menu at the bottom of the pane to choose relevant commands, as shown in Figure 6.3. This is a quick way to duplicate the Stop field, edit it, and rename it from Stop 1 to Start.

As you drag each field, you see it travel beneath your mouse; it also shows up in the place where Bento places it so you can drop it in the exact location you want.

Figure 6.3   *Use the shortcuts menu.*

Using Date and Time Field Controls

Date and time fields have small calendar and clock icons to their right, which we get into in this section. Before moving on, however, make sure you check that the fields are properly formatted so that there is space for these icons. Figure 6.4 shows how you can drag the right side of a field to adjust its width; Bento displays a guide when you are in the right position. Before moving on, click the calendar to enter a date and time. If the field is not wide enough, enlarge both Start and Stop fields so the text can be accommodated.

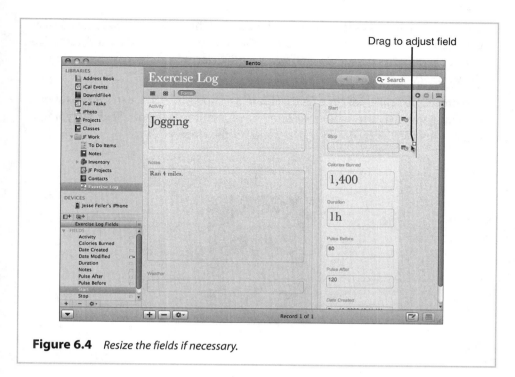

Figure 6.4   *Resize the fields if necessary.*

From the user's point of view, these controls provide fast data entry. Figure 6.5 shows the calendar in action for a date field.

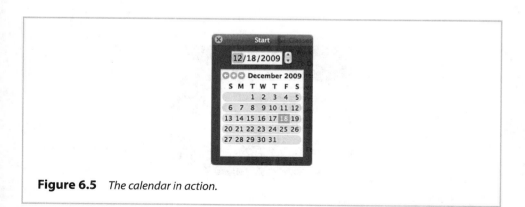

Figure 6.5   *The calendar in action.*

You open the calendar by clicking the small calendar icon next to a date field. Then you can navigate through the calendar using either the number at the top and the up and down arrows or the arrows at the upper right. To select a date, you click it. If you then close the calendar, that date is placed in the associated field. Alternatively, double-click the date you want; the calendar closes, and the date is entered in the field.

The process is similar for time fields. Figure 6.6 shows how you can set the time: with up and down arrows for a selected hour, minute, or am/pm field; by typing into those fields; or by dragging the hands of the clock.

Figure 6.6   *Set time values.*

Finally, for a date field that includes the option for time, a composite tool is automatically provided, as shown in Figure 6.7.

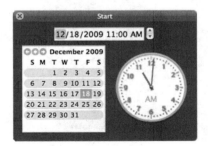

Figure 6.7   *A composite date/time field in action.*

Creating and Formatting a Number Field in Exercise Log

You now need to create a Calories Rate field that will be used in calculating the calories burned for your exercise time. This number field will contain the rate at which calories are burned per hour for this exercise.

You can work from the sample data in the Exercise Log library, which shows 1,400 calories burned in one hour of exercising. To start, you can use this value, but you should check any of the various exercise calculators you can find on the Web (search for "calorie rate counter") because the true value depends on the specific exercise as well as your body weight.

Figure 6.8 shows how you create a number field.

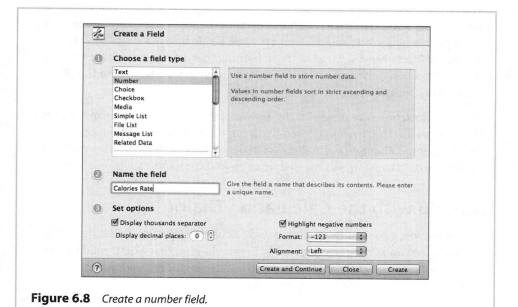

Figure 6.8   *Create a number field.*

Your options are shown at the bottom of the dialog. You can choose whether to display a thousands separator (what it is depends on your International settings in System Preferences) and how many decimal places to use. Note that these are for display of the data in the field. If you choose not to display a thousands separator and type in 123,456,789, Bento accepts it and displays it as 123456789.

If you choose to highlight negative numbers, they are shown in red. You can also choose a format for negative numbers: –123 or (123). Finally, you can choose whether the number (positive or negative) is aligned to the right or left of the field. In general, when numbers are displayed vertically, right alignment looks best because that is how people normally write them and use them when they are adding them up.

After you have created your field, drag it into the form.

 SHOW ME   Media 6.2—A video about creating a date/time field
Access this video file through your registered Web Edition at
my.safaribooksonline.com/9780131388611/media.

Creating and Formatting Calculations in Exercise Log

Bento calculation fields let you create calculations that combine data in other fields with constant (unchanging values (such as pi) and with changing but known values outside Bento databases (such as the current date). You can also create calculations or formulas inside spreadsheet cells and inside fields of databases such as FileMaker Pro or Access. Some of those formulas can become complex; they can even include major programming techniques such as transfers of control (if/then statements, for example), temporary variables, and more.

Bento's calculations are powerful and simple. If you are used to thinking in procedural terms (do this, then that, then the other thing...), Bento calculations are different. Like Bento libraries (and databases in general), they describe a formula or relationship that is evaluated as needed from the data at hand.

Working with the Calculation Dialog

In this section, you see how to create two calculation fields based on the fields in the Exercise Log as modified previously in this chapter. First, you should become familiar with the Calculation dialog. When you create a new field, you can choose its type to be Calculation, as shown in Figure 6.2.

Next, you see the Calculation dialog that lets you name the field (just as you always do), specify the calculation, and set the type of the result, as shown in Figure 6.9.

As always, Bento attempts to convert fields of one type to another as needed. In Bento and any other database, it is best to use the most specific type for a given field. You can store dates in text fields, for example, but only date fields can take advantage of Bento's automatic date formatting and simplified date entry.

In the lower left of the dialog shown in Figure 6.9, you can click Show Examples. This flips the dialog to its back, and you see examples of calculations, as shown in Figure 6.10.

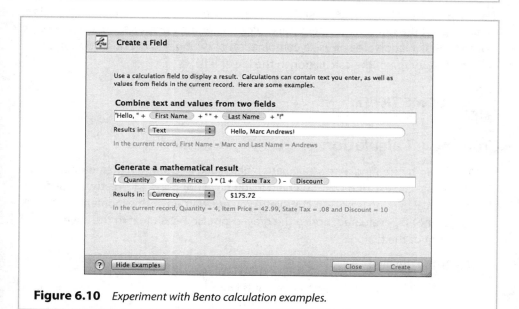

Figure 6.9   *Name the field and set its result type.*

Figure 6.10   *Experiment with Bento calculation examples.*

This dialog is live: You can modify the text in the two calculations and see the result in the field just below each of the two calculations. You can also adjust the result's type so that you can see how Bento changes the result.

Flip the dialog back to the front by clicking Hide Examples. Now you are ready to create your calculation fields.

Creating the Duration Field

The Exercise Log library has a Duration field into which you can type the duration of your exercise using the standard Bento duration symbols (h/hour, m/minutes, s/seconds—even the most ardent exercise is unlikely to need d/day in the Duration field, but it is there if necessary).

Now that you have both a Start and Stop field in the library, you can create a new Duration field that is a calculation. Delete the existing Duration field and begin to create a new one by clicking the + at the bottom of the Fields pane or choosing Insert > New Field. Select Calculation for the field type.

> **NOTE**
> Now that you have created a number of fields, the details of using the + at the bottom of the Fields pane or Insert > New Field are omitted for the balance of the book.

The simplest way to create a calculation is to select each field in the calculation in turn from the list and either double-click or click Insert to move it into the calculation area at the right. Where necessary, click one of the operators. You can also type into the calculation area or use a combination of typing and clicking. You can specify the result type of the calculation in the lower left.

 **LET ME TRY IT**

Creating a Calculation

1. Begin by creating a new calculation field such as Duration. (Remember to delete the existing Duration field if you have not done so already. Because the calculation is not yet complete, you are warned at this moment that it cannot be evaluated: notice the grayed-out No Result text in the lower right of the dialog.

2. Name the field.

3. Select the result type (in this case it is Duration).

4. Build the formula from the fields in the Available Field list. Use the operators in the center of the dialog to do this. You want Stop – Start in this case.

5. If you have entered data, watch the result that is calculated in the lower right as shown in Figure 6.12. If you do not have data in the fields of the current record, click Create to create the new calculation field and then

enter some data in the Start and Stop fields. (You can use the calendar icons to quickly select the current date and time for each. You may want to move the Start time value back an hour or two to make the duration calculation more significant.)

6. Click OK to complete the calculation.

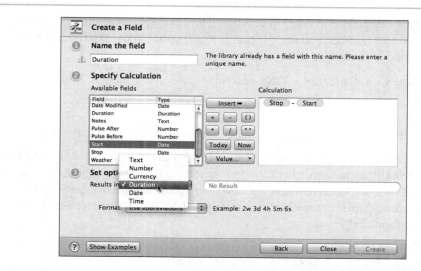

Figure 6.11   *Create the calculation.*

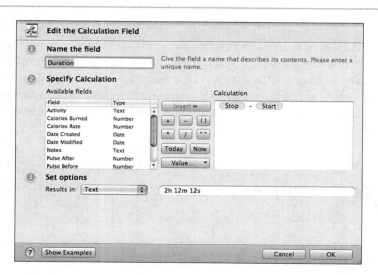

Figure 6.12   *Bento evaluates the calculation based on data in the current record.*

SHOW ME   Media 6.3—A video about creating a calculation
Access this video file through your registered Web Edition at
my.safaribooksonline.com/9780131388611/media.

Experiment with changing the result type to see how that influences the result.

Bento stores all dates and times in seconds. If you change the result type of this calculation to a number, you see the number of seconds in the duration. For this set of data, the numeric value is 7,932:

- 2 hours = 120 minutes = 7,200 seconds
- 12 minutes = 720 seconds
- 12 seconds

Complete the process of creating the Duration field by dragging the new field from the Fields list into the form. Check the format setting (Shading and Text Size) of Duration Old to make certain that the new field's settings match. Experiment by entering some data into the new Start and Stop fields. The Duration field should update automatically.

Creating the Calories Burned Field

Now that you have the new Duration field created as a calculation and you have the Calorie Rate field created as a number, you can create the main calculation: Calories Burned.

The simplest way to begin is by deleting the existing Calories Burned field that was included in the form by default: You will replace it with the calculation. Then make certain that you have a value entered in the new Calorie Rate field. To make your testing as simple as possible, adjust the Start and Stop fields to be exactly one hour apart. For Calorie Rate, enter 1,400 (the value the sample record has in the built-in library).

NOTE
Whether or not you use a comma is up to you—Bento is equally happy with 1400 or 1,400.

Now create a Calories Burned calculation field. With those values, you can enter a calculation of Calorie Rate * Duration, as shown in Figure 6.13.

Now your modified Exercise Log calculates duration and calories burned. Along the way, you have seen how to use calculations and how to use Date, Time, and

Date/Time fields. The balance of this chapter explores other commonly used fields in Bento.

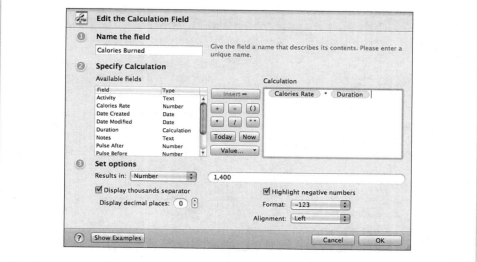

Figure 6.13 *Create the Calories Burned calculation.*

Creating and Formatting Choice Fields

Choice fields are displayed to the user in a pop-up menu when he or she accesses a choice field. The user can select a single value from that menu.

When you create the choice field, you must provide at least one choice. You can use – for a choice on a line by itself, which creates a separator in the pop-up menu. Figure 6.14 shows how to set the choice values. You can select a row and use + or – to add a new row beneath it or to delete it. You can also click directly on a line and enter a value. To rearrange the choices, just click one and drag it up or down to its new position.

Choice fields work best when the number of choices is less than 20. (Some inter-face designers would suggest a dozen as a maximum.) If you have more choices, you have to scroll through too many values to find what you want and even to know what is available. You can minimize this problem by arranging the choices in groups with separators, but you might want to consider using a text field with the type-ahead option so that as you type, previously entered values are shown.

Beginning with Bento 3, there is always a blank choice at the top of the pop-up menu. Users who have previously selected a choice value can use this blank choice to remove that value without choosing another one.

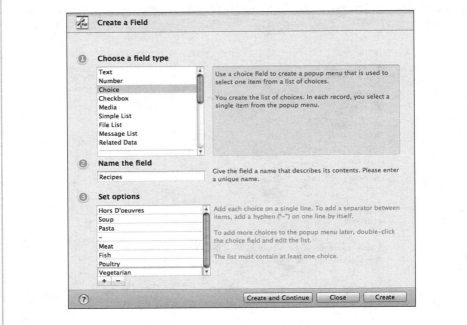

Figure 6.14 *Enter choice values.*

Creating and Formatting Checkbox Fields

A checkbox field consists of a checkbox and some text, which is the field name. Examples are status information such as Verified, Completed, or In Progress. Bento checkboxes have a slightly different functionality than other checkboxes because you can either check a checkbox or not check it: The values are Yes and No. Sometimes that Yes/No structure does not fit the data easily. For example, if you want to keep track of gender, you can use a choice field with values Male and Female. If you use a checkbox field, you would have to name it either Male or Female. The records checked would be Male (or Female), and the other gender would consist of any record that is not checked.

Status, too, often lends itself to a choice field so that you can change it from Not Started to In Progress to Completed. If you use a checkbox, you work with the single value (such as Finished).

> **NOTE**
> Choice and checkbox fields are good ways of storing data, but they are also excellent ways of organizing data. You can search your library for a specific checkbox value to limit the records you are looking at (Not Finished, for

example). In Chapter 7, "Expanding the Inventory Library with Related Records and Collections," you see how you can use a checkbox or choice field to drive the whole process of maintaining a Smart Collection.

Creating and Formatting Currency Fields

Currency fields are a special type of number field. You set them up as shown in Figure 6.15. You can choose the currency symbol to use. In Figure 6.15, you can see that the currently selected value is the Zimbabwe Dollars (Z$). When the mouse is released, the symbol changes to the Euro (€).

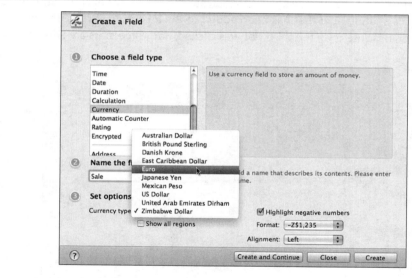

Figure 6.15 *Set options for a currency field.*

The checkbox to show all regions provides you with a much longer list of currency symbols (and is an example of how lengthy choice fields can be problematic).

As with number fields, if you highlight negative numbers, they are shown in color. Also, as with number fields, you can align the currency value left or right.

Creating and Formatting Automatic Counter Fields

An automatic counter is used to provide a number for each record. You specify the number to be used for the next record and the increment to be used, and Bento takes care of everything.

For example, if you start at 1 with an increment of 1, the automatic counter fields for the first 5 records are 1, 2, 3, 4, and 5. If you start at 20 with an increment of 5, the values are 20, 25, 30, and so forth.

In many databases, it is critically important to have primary keys with unique values that you can use in creating relationships. In Bento, the entire mechanism of relationships is managed for you without having to create keys, so you do not have to worry about it.

Creating and Formatting Rating Fields

Finally, you can create a rating field. You give it a name and indicate the rating values to be used—you can go up to 10. Then, as shown in Figure 6.16, dots appear for the values, and you can click a dot to indicate the rating. For example, the Popularity field is a rating field that has been added to the Inventory library. It allows five values; in Figure 6.16, the third dot was clicked, and three stars are shown.

Figure 6.16 *Use a rating field.*

Editing Bento Fields

You can change the name of a field and change its options by double-clicking it in the Fields pane, or you can choose Edit from the Actions icon below the Fields pane. This can be particularly useful with choice fields: you can change the contents of the choice field's popup menu in this way, as shown in Figure 6.17.

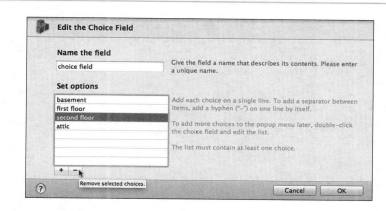

Figure 6.17   *Edit a choice field.*

If you delete a choice, as shown here, those values remain in the field. So if you have a record in which second floor is selected (that is the choice about to be deleted), those values remain. In the pop-up menu displaying choice values for those records, second floor is still visible. It is not visible in other records.

You can also change the type of a Bento field by selecting it and using the Actions icon as shown in Figure 6.18. Your choices in this shortcuts menu vary depending on the type of the field you are changing. For example, text fields can be changed to almost any other type (choice fields are basically text fields). Rating fields can only be changed to text, number, and choice fields. Picture fields cannot be changed to any other type. As long as you understand the principle, the actual possibilities make sense. Some conversions may be a two-step process, such as Date to Text and then Text to Rating. In the process, Bento may warn you about data loss, and you must take the responsibility for converting dates to ratings, which are very different data types.

In table view, you can use the triangle at the right of a column header to access all available commands for that field, including changing its type, as shown in Figure 6.19. Note that the example shown in Figure 6.19 converts all of the values in the Category field to values in the new Category field, which is now a Choice field. Each record retains its value, but if you click in a Category field after the change, you will see a pop-up menu with all of the current values displayed.

TELL ME MORE   **Media 6.4—A discussion about changing field types**

Access this audio recording through your registered Web Edition at **my.safaribooksonline.com/9780131388611/media.**

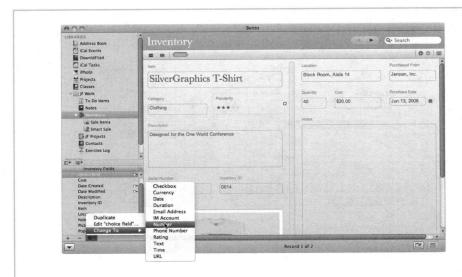

Figure 6.18 *Change the type of a text field.*

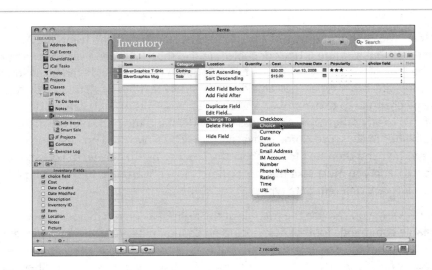

Figure 6.19 *Change a field's type in table view.*

7

Expanding the Inventory Library with Related Data Fields and Collections

This chapter will show you how to use relationships and collections to organize your Bento data.

Exploring the Inventory Library

Just as the Exercise Log was used in the last chapter to demonstrate the use of various Bento fields, the Inventory library is used in this chapter to explore concepts of related records and collections. Inventory is one of the built-in Bento libraries. In its basic state, it lets you keep track of inventory items. You can see the basic library in Figure 7.1. Note that the picture and notes fields have been slightly reduced in size for the figure.

Using the Inventory library, you can enter names, prices, codes, and so forth. In the Picture field at the lower left of the form shown in Figure 7.1, you can add an image or video clip of the product. This is a standard Bento media field. As you have seen with fields such as the date and time fields, Bento automatically provides interface tools for media fields. For example, when you click in an empty media field, you see the controls shown in Figure 7.2. These controls let you either insert an existing file or, if you have a built-in iSight camera, you can take a picture right on the spot that Bento adds to the field.

When a picture is in the field, the controls shown in Figure 7.3 are available. You can save the picture to disk, change its size, or fit it to the frame. If you drag a movie into a media field, it has standard media controls available.

There are some similarities between the Inventory library and the Exercise Log library that was used as an example in Chapter 6, "Working with Bento Fields and Calculations." In both cases, you can enter data directly into the libraries. And in both cases you can make data entry much simpler by using some of Bento's features. In the preceding chapter, you saw how calculation fields could help by calculating values from your inputs you accomplish organization and tracking goals.

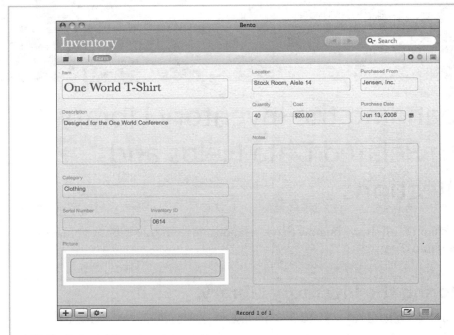

Figure 7.1 *Explore the Inventory library.*

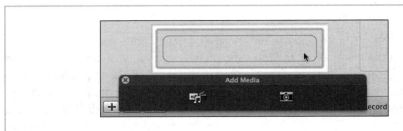

Figure 7.2 *Use the media field.*

In this chapter, you see how you can use another Bento feature to simplify data entry—the Quantity field. Rather than simply entering quantity in the field, Bento enables you to set up the Inventory library so that you can enter additions and subtractions to the quantity on hand as you buy more inventory and sell items. At first you might think this is another calculation, but a calculation requires that you have the component elements available in each database record. (Although elements that are constants or predefined values such as today's date obviously do not need to be present in the record.) What you need to do to in this case is to create another library with its own set of records that can keep track of the additions and subtractions to your inventory ("Ins & Outs," as some people call them). Then you need to be able to relate that library to the Inventory library. If you have ever done this in a traditional database, you know that it isn't particularly difficult. You just set up a field in one table that matches with a field in the other table and then fill in the proper values, making certain that they remain synchronized.

It's even easier in Bento.

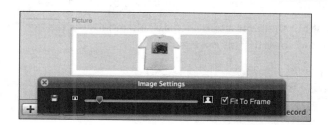

Figure 7.3   *Control the media field.*

Creating an Ins & Outs Library from Scratch

Although there are several types of database relationships, the most common one that you use in Bento is one in which a single record in the main table (perhaps representing an inventory item) is related to records in the related table (such as Ins & Outs). Bento manages the mechanics of this for you. There are three logical possibilities based on the number of Ins & Outs records that are related to a single inventory record:

- Zero. If there are no Ins & Outs records, no transactions have occurred. The inventory item exists in the main table, but with no transactions, its inventory level is zero.

- One. If there is a single record in the Ins & Outs table, it represents the inventory level for the item.

- More than one. If there are several records in the Ins & Outs table, the inventory level for the item is the sum of all of the quantities in the related Ins & Outs table (2 items sold yesterday, 5 received today, 1 item sold today, and so forth).

If you have the related library, it is just a matter of connecting it to the main table (you will see how to do this in the next section). However, you may need to create the related library from scratch.

To add inventory transactions to the Inventory library, you need to create a new library from the Blank template for the ins and outs—the additions to and subtractions from inventory—which requires three fields:

- Quantity in or out (positive numbers represent additions to inventory, or ins, and negative numbers represent subtractions, or outs). This is a number field.

- Date of the transaction, which should be a date field.

- Notes about the transaction such as "sold at farmers' market," "bought from co-op," and so forth. This is a text field.

 **LET ME TRY IT**

Creating an Ins & Outs Library

1. Start by creating a new library from the Blank template using File > New Library From Template or the + beneath the Libraries pane. Name it Ins & Outs.

2. You are now in table view with the two default fields created, as shown in Figure 7.4. (They are in the Fields pane, but not added to the table view unless you do so.)

3. Create the quantity field. Double-click the header for the first column that is set by default to New Field. As soon as you click in that header, its name immediately changes to Field 1. At the same time, a new column titled New Field is provided to the right so that you can enter the next field. Just type into the header to change Field 1 to Quantity.

4. Use the triangle next to the name to change the field's type to Number, as shown in Figure 7.5.

5. Repeat the process for Date and Notes. In the case of notes, you do not have to edit the field: The default field type is text, which is what you want.

 **SHOW ME**   Media 7.1—A video about creating an Ins & Outs library
Access this video file through your registered Web Edition at
my.safaribooksonline.com/9780131388611/media.

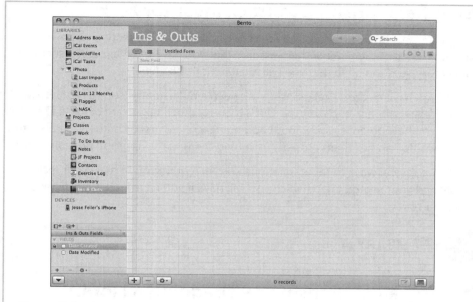

Figure 7.4 *Create Ins & Outs.*

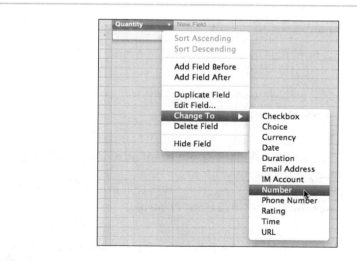

Figure 7.5 *Edit the field to make it a number.*

The mechanism for creating the relationship between Inventory and Ins & Outs is the next step in the process.

Using Relationships to Track Inventory

There are several ways to create a relationship in Bento. This section walks you through each of them. All of them assume that you have the main table (such as Inventory) and the table that you will relate to it (Ins & Outs).

Once you have created a relationship between a main library (such as Inventory) and a related library (such as Ins & Outs) it pretty much takes care of itself. The only thing you have to do is worry about adding new related records (Ins & Outs) — the relationship handles them properly assigning them to the appropriate main record.

Here are several ways to set up relationships. All require you to have your main table and your related table (which you will have if you have worked through this chapter so far).

 **LET ME TRY IT**

Creating a Relationship by Dragging a Library onto a Form

You can create a relationship by dragging the library to be related into a form of the main library.

1. Open the Inventory library in one of its forms.

2. Drag Ins & Outs from the Libraries pane onto the form, as shown in Figure 7.6.

3. The relationship is created when you release the mouse button (see Figure 7.7). You see a small table view in the form.

 SHOW ME   Media 7.2—A video about creating a relationship by dragging a library onto a form
Access this video file through your registered Web Edition at
my.safaribooksonline.com/9780131388611/media.

By default, the fields in the related records field are those that are in the table view of the related library, but you can add other fields or remove them from the related data field view if you want.

The Fields pane at the bottom of the Libraries & Fields pane is rearranged. As shown in Figure 7.7, a related data field shows the related library (there can be any number of these for your main library if you have a more complex design).

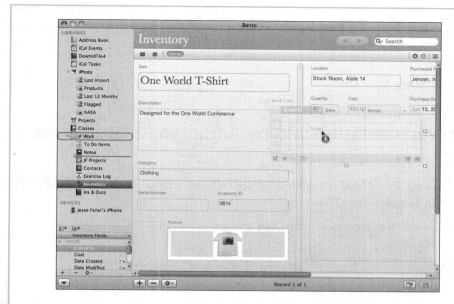

Figure 7.6 *Create a relationship by dragging a library onto a form.*

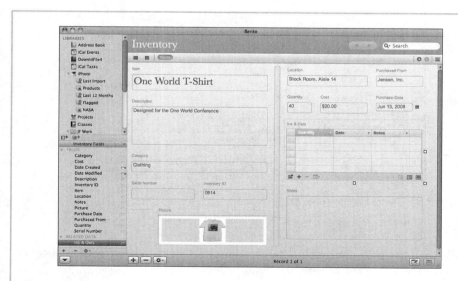

Figure 7.7 *Bento separates related data from local fields in the Fields pane.*

When you drag a library onto a form, it is related to the form's library, and, as noted in the previous section, a related data field is created in the form's library. You can also add a related data field directly as described here.

 **LET ME TRY IT**

Creating a Relationship by Adding a Related Data Field

1. Create a new field in the main library with the + below the fields pane or with Insert > New Field.

2. Set the field type to Related Data and name it Ins & Outs, as shown in Figure 7.8.

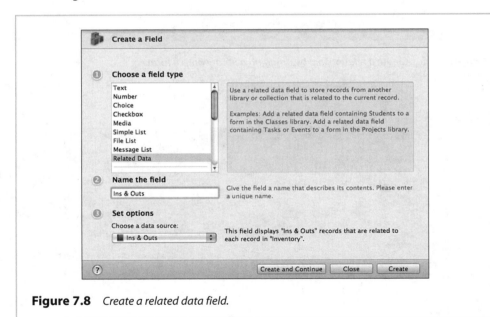

Figure 7.8 *Create a related data field.*

3. The pop-up Options menu that lets you choose a data source automatically contains all of the libraries you have in Bento, as shown in Figure 7.9.

If you use this approach, the related records list field is created in the Fields pane, and you can then add it to your form as you would any other field.

Figure 7.9   *Choose a data source for the related data field.*

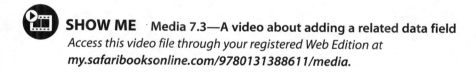

SHOW ME   Media 7.3—A video about adding a related data field
Access this video file through your registered Web Edition at
my.safaribooksonline.com/9780131388611/media.

Formatting the Related Data Field

The related records in a related data field are shown in a related data field as you saw previously in Figure 7.7. You can format the related records list much like any other field (although you cannot change its text size). One special formatting feature is important to use such a field properly. If you click the button in the lower right corner of the related records list, you can change the display in the Fields pane to be the fields in the related record field, not the fields in the main library, as shown in Figure 7.10. Click the fields in the Fields list that you want to be shown in the related records list field, just as you would to specify the fields for a table view. To rearrange the fields, just drag the column headers back and forth until they are in the order you want. You can also resize the columns.

Just as in a table view, you can rearrange the columns in a related data field, but you can also use the triangle at the top of each column to sort a column or hide it. This is shown in Figure 7.11.

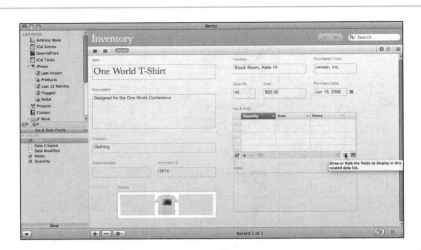

Figure 7.10 *Select the fields to be shown in the related data field.*

Figure 7.11 *Column headers in related data fields work the same as they do in table view.*

 **LET ME TRY IT**

Adding Data to a Related Data Field

Now you are ready to start using the related records.

1. To add a record use the + at the lower left of the related data field to add a row.

2. Use the – to delete the selected row.

 SHOW ME Media 7.4—A video about adding data to a related field
Access this video file through your registered Web Edition at
my.safaribooksonline.com/9780131388611/media.

Remember that when you add a record to the related data field, you use the + at the lower left of that field. To add a new record to the main library, you use the + at the bottom of the window just as you would do in any library.

 LET ME TRY IT

Adding a Related Data Field and its Data

You can add a related data field and its data in one step.

1. Make certain you have at least one record in your main library and at least one in your library to be related.

2. Open the library to be related in table view.

3. Select the record(s) you want to relate to the main table.

4. Drag them onto the library icon in the Libraries pane.

5. You will be asked which record you want to relate them to in the main library as shown in Figure 7.12.

Note that you can relate the data to more than one record in the main table, but more often you want to relate the related records to one record (such as many transactions for a single product).

 SHOW ME Media 7.5—A video about adding a related data field
and its data
Access this video file through your registered Web Edition at
my.safaribooksonline.com/9780131388611/media.

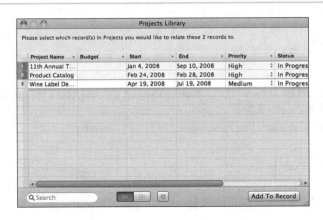

Figure 7.12 *Select the record(s) to relate the data to.*

Summarizing a Related Data Field

At the lower right of a related data field is the button to show or hide the summary row. Just as you can with a table, you can choose from sum, average, and other functions depending on the field type. Show the summary row and select Sum for the summary function of the quantity column. (If it is not shown in the related records list field, click in the field and click the checkbox in the Fields list for the related library next to Quantity.)

Notice that as you enter the data, the summary row is updated with the ins (positive numbers) and outs (negative numbers). Instead of the static Quantity field in the built-in template, you now have a live inventory tracker, as shown in Figure 7.13.

Reviewing the Related Records

If you go to the Ins & Outs library, you will see that the records you have entered through the related records list in Inventory are in the Ins & Outs library. While you are in the Ins & Outs library, try adding another record to it. Then go back to the Inventory library, where you will see that the new record you added to Ins & Outs is not shown in the related records list field in Inventory.

The reason this new record isn't shown is that the only records from Ins & Outs shown in that list field are those that were entered through that Inventory record: They are the related records. If you go to another Inventory record, the related records list field only shows the Ins & Outs records that were entered through the second Inventory record. Bento keeps track of all this so that everything works as it should and you do not have to worry about it.

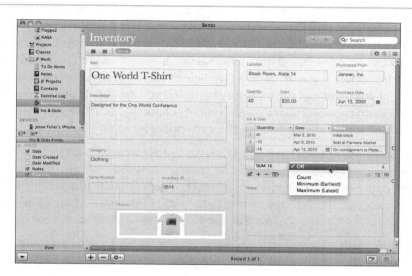

Figure 7.13   *Enter data in the related library.*

Bento keeps track of which records in the related library are related to which other library and to which record in the library. Records entered through Inventory show up in the full Ins & Outs library as well as in the Inventory related records list field of the record through which they were entered. You can relate a given library to any number of other records. In addition to Inventory, you might create a library called Production that keeps track of your manufacturing of items. You can relate Ins & Outs to Production as well as Inventory.

CAUTION

If you delete a record from Ins & Outs—the basic library that is related to Inventory, Production, and maybe other libraries—that record is deleted everywhere. It is the basic library that stores the data; everything else stores references to the data, and if that original data is gone, that is the end of it. A warning dialog appears when you are about to do this, but even the most experienced users occasionally delete records that are needed in related tables. That is why Bento backups are so important.

Improving the Relationship and the Form

You can remove the old Quantity field from the Inventory library to clean things up because it is no longer needed because the summary row shows the current sum of Ins & Outs, which is the dynamic quantity on hand.

While you are thinking about removing the Quantity field, take a look at the other fields in that part of the form: Purchased From, Cost, and Purchase Date. You already have a date field in the Ins & Outs related record. The notes field can be used to store the purchased from information, or you can add a Purchased From field to Ins & Outs. If you also add a Cost field to Ins & Outs, you have all the information in this section of the Inventory form, and you are able to store multiple values reflecting costs and suppliers for a variety of purchases. While you are at it, you might want to add a Price field to reflect the prices for sales.

If you add these fields to Ins & Outs, they are not automatically added to the related data field. However, you can use the same process you used in setting up the related data field field to add them. Select the related data field and click the icon at the lower right to show the related data fields.) Click the checkboxes next to the items you want to have displayed and then rearrange and resize the columns.

With those fields removed, you can rearrange the form, as shown in Figure 7.14.

Figure 7.14 *Rearrange the form.*

You might have several sets of related records. In addition to Ins & Outs, you might have a list of vendors for the item or maybe a list of colors or sizes in which the item is available. There is no limit to the number of related data fields you can have in a Bento library.

There are a few restrictions on the use of related data fields, though. One is that the visible fields for a given related data field apply to all occurrences of that field. If the related data field is shown on several forms, all the fields for that related data field show the fields set on any of the forms.

TIP

Although Bento handles relationships quite simply, in adding relationships to your libraries, you need to remember what the relationships are. Building a number of relationships might make your Bento library harder to use. Remember, too, that relationships in Bento are always one step long. If you have a library called A that is related to a library called B, creating a relationship from a new library to A creates no relationship to B.

An icon at the bottom of the related data field lets you go to the record you have clicked, as shown in Figure 7.15. It opens in the last display you used for the related data—be it the table or grid view or one of the form views.

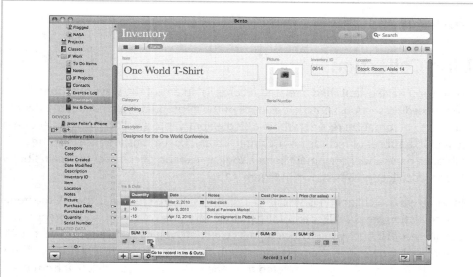

Figure 7.15   *Go to a related record.*

Once you have gone to the related record, a back button appears in the navigation bar that lets you return to the original record, as shown in Figure 7.16.

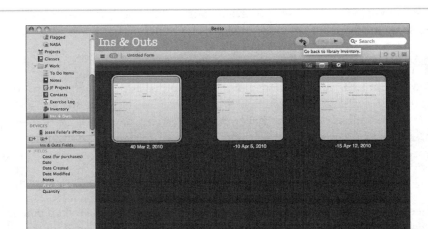

Figure 7.16 *Return to the original record.*

Using Collections

When you have established a related records list in any of the ways described in the preceding section, Bento keeps track of the appropriate related records. Bento also lets you organize records within a single library into a collection. A collection is just that: a subset of records from a single library. Collections are shown in the Libraries pane under their main library. You can expand or contract the main library to see its collections, as shown in Figure 7.17.

In some ways, a collection is similar to a relationship. The reason is that all the items in a collection are actually part of the main library. The collection is a reference to certain records. After you have created a collection, you can add a record to it, and that record shows up in the main library (which is actually where it is stored). If you delete it from the library, it is deleted from the collection. If you delete it from the collection, a dialog lets you choose whether to delete it from both the collection and main library or just from the collection.

The rules for collections are much like those for relationships:

- You can have any number of collections within a library.

- The same record can be in any number of collections within a library.

In the example shown in Figure 7.16, a collection has been set up for Sale Items from Inventory. You can see it in the Libraries pane at the left directly underneath its parent library and slightly indented. You can use the disclosure triangle for the parent library to show or hide its collection. The Sale Items records are still in the Inventory table, but they are collected together. Other such collections might be new items, discontinued items, and so forth. Using collections provides a further way of organizing your Bento data.

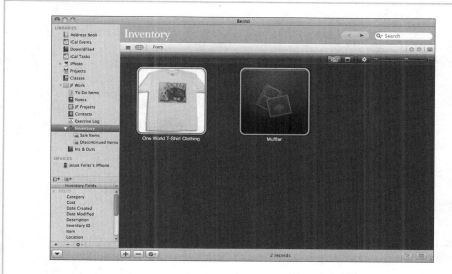

Figure 7.17   *Use collections.*

Creating an Empty Collection

The simplest way to create a new collection is to choose File > New Collection or to use Add Collection, as shown in Figure 7.18.

This action creates a new collection inside the main library. Whether you have selected the main library itself (Inventory in this case) or another collection within it, the collection is created. All collections for a library are placed under its name; you can rearrange them by dragging them up or down. At first each new collection is given an untitled name; you should change it immediately to something like Sale Items. As is the case with renaming any library, just click the name in the Libraries pane and type the new name.

Adding a Record to a Collection

When you have a collection, you can add records to it. Just select the collection and click the Add Record button from the Records area or choose Records > New Record; this adds a record to the collection and, of course, to the main library as well.

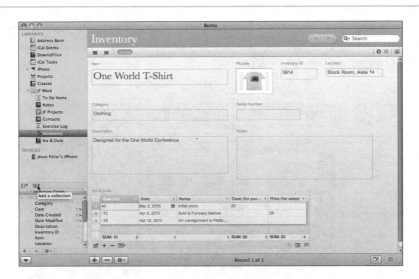

Figure 7.18 *Add a new empty collection.*

If you already have a record, you can add it to any collection within that library. Navigate to the record and choose Add to Collection from the Additional Commands button, as shown in Figure 7.19. (You can also choose Edit > Add To to select the collection to which you want to add it.) If you choose multiple records from a table or grid view, you can add all of them at once to a collection in the same way.

You can also simply drag the selected record(s) from a table or grid view into a collection. It's no coincidence that this is the same way in which you can add a song to a playlist in iTunes: it uses the same programming and user interface techniques.

Creating a Collection from Selected Records

You can combine both steps if you want to create a collection from a set of records that you have selected. Select the records in table or grid view or navigate to the specific record from which you want to create a collection. Then choose New Collection from Selection as shown in Figure 7.20. You are prompted to name the collection, and then it is created. After that, you can manually add records to the collection as described in the previous section.

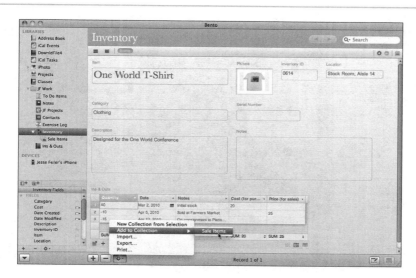

Figure 7.19   *Add a record to a collection.*

Using Smart Collections

Collections are a simple way to organize your data in any way that you want. But Bento also provides you with Smart Collections. This is the same type of Smart technology that you see in the Finder with Smart Folders and in a variety of other places in Mac OS X.

A Smart Collection consists of an Advanced Find query that selects certain records. The Smart Collection always displays the records that satisfy that query: You do not have to do anything to update the Smart Collection. If a new record's data qualifies it for the Smart Collection, it is part of the Smart Collection. If a change to the record's data disqualifies it, it disappears from the Smart Collection, but it remains in the main library unless you delete it.

🄖 *Smart Collections are based on Advanced Find. This is described in detail in Chapter 2, "Using the Bento Window," p. 25.*

There are two ways of creating a Smart Collection. If you are working with an Advanced Find, the Save button at the upper right corner of the window creates a Smart Collection based on that query. Click Save and then enter a name for the Smart Collection, and you're set.

Alternatively, you can choose File > New Smart Collection. This opens Advanced Find so that you can create the query and then click Save.

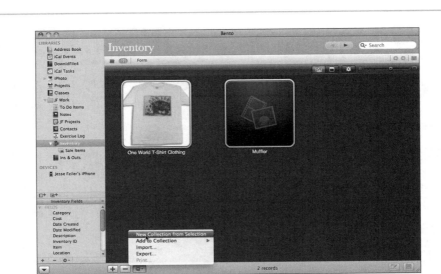

Figure 7.20 *Create a new collection from a selection in grid or table view.*

Here is an example. Instead of manually creating a Sale Items collection, you can mark items as being in the sale category. To do this, add a Merchandise field that uses the choice field type.

Figure 7.21 shows how you can set this field in any record in Inventory.

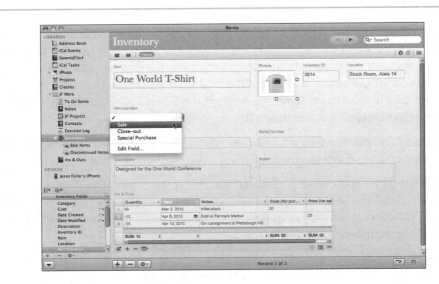

Figure 7.21 *Set the field values as necessary.*

Now, using the techniques for advanced search as described in Chapter 2, create a query that searches for "sale" in the Merchandise field, as shown in Figure 7.22.

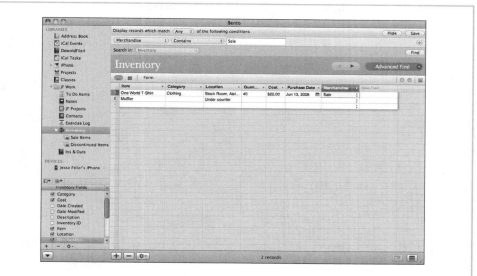

Figure 7.22   *Create the Smart Collection.*

Now click Save in the upper right corner of the window to create the Smart Collection. You can rename it something meaningful such as Smart Sale. Now, move through the library and change the Merchandise field on various records to Sale or to other categories. Whenever you change the Sale value on a record, it is added to or deleted from the Smart Sale collection as necessary.

> **NOTE**
>
> Any time you can make a process automatic, your Bento database (like any other database) is more stable. Like related records, Smart Collections rely on data entry and data entry alone for creating links or collections; you do not have to remember to do a second step. Also note that you can set up the Smart Collection even if there are no records that fulfill the advanced find query. Just set up the query and click Save. Thereafter, when records have the required data value, they will appear in the Smart Collection.

8

Synchronizing with the Bento iPhone and iPad Apps

In this chapter you learn how to use the Bento iPhone and iPad apps to synchronize your data between your iPhone or iPad and your Mac.

The first two versions of Bento were stand-alone applications, a truly personal database for one user and one computer. In this chapter and the next one you see how Bento has blossomed into a sharable database. It is still a personal database, and it still is centered on a single user, but you can now share and synchronize Bento libraries over a local area network as well as with an iPhone or iPad. Mobile synchronization, the topic of this chapter, is accomplished with the Bento app that you buy (for $4.99) from the Apple iTunes App store. Sharing, the topic of the next chapter, is built into Bento and it lets you use a Bento library on several locally networked computers.

> **NOTE**
> As you will see from the Bento interface commands, synchronization is referred to as being between Bento on your Mac and a "device." At this time, such devices consist of iPhone, iPod touch, and iPad.

Sharing Versus Synchronization

These two concepts are related but quite different, and they are not specific to Bento although this discussion focuses on Bento. *Sharing* means being able to use a single Bento library from two or more devices at the same time. (There is a Bento limit of five.) The shared library is located on a computer, which allows other computers to connect to it. If the computer on which the library is located is not available, no other computer can connect to the library because that is the only place where the library is located.

(Bento uses a different type of sharing when it accesses your Address Book, Photos, and iCal data. This data is located on your computer along with the Bento database containing your libraries, but the actual data resides only in Address Book, iPhoto, and iCal. Bento accesses that data uses application programming interface (API) calls that Apple provides to developers.)

Sharing happens in real time, with multiple users simultaneously accessing the database. (In reality update accesses to shared databases are not simultaneous—one always precedes another, but for most people most of the time, the appearance is simultaneous.)

Synchronization lets you update multiple copies of a library on multiple computers; the synchronization process compares the changes and merges the latest ones together. The synchronization process requires that both copies of a library on both devices be accessible at the time of synchronization. In practical terms, this means that Bento must be running on your computer and on your mobile device at the time you are synchronizing.

Because there are multiple copies of the data involved, synchronization can occur at any time both copies can be accessed. The process, though, does not provide immediate synchronization. For that reason, as soon as synchronization has occurred, both copies of the data can be accessed and updated on their respective devices. This allows the data on each device to be inconsistent with the data on another device, but the next synchronization process resolves those inconsistencies.

In some cases, the data in the separate devices is not just generally inconsistent (a To Do item may exist on your computer's Bento database, and another To Do item may exist on your iPhone). You could have five To Do items on your computer and five on your iPhone, but while four of them might be identical, the fifth on each device might be different. After synchronization, you will have six To Do items on both your iPhone and your computer.

When you synchronize iCal or Address Book data on your computer with MobileMe, you are asked about resolving conflicts within specific items: If you have two versions of an address or phone number or two times for a specific event, you can choose which one you want to use. Bento synchronization for iPhone simplifies this process. In cases of conflicting data, the iPhone data in a Bento library overwrites the corresponding data on your computer.

It is important to note that you can synchronize multiple devices with MobileMe and, through MobileMe, with one another. Bento synchronization is between your Mac and your mobile device, just as your synchronization for iTunes is for one mobile device/Mac combination. You can change the device for a given Bento installation (and vice versa), but at any point in time, only one pairing is allowed.

> **TIP**
>
> Because synchronization can change the data on both your mobile device and your computer, always begin by backup up both devices.

Using the Bento iPhone or iPad App by Itself

The Bento iPhone and iPad apps are separate products from Bento. You can buy them from the link at http://www.filemaker.com/products/bento/iphone.html and install it as you would any app. You can use it on its own even if you do not use Bento, but its value is greatly increased if you synchronize it with your Bento data.

When you open the Bento iPhone app, you will find four buttons across the bottom of the screen:

- Home
- Search
- New Library
- Sync & Setup

On iPad, these functions are provided as part of the basic interface without using a toolbar at the bottom of the screen.

The first three are described in this section. Sync & Setup is described later in this chapter.

Using the Bento iPad App

Figure 8.1 shows you the basic layout of the Bento iPad app. At the left, a list of libraries lets you choose which one to look at. On the right, you see the data for that library.

If you tap one of the libraries in the list, you can see its records and select the one you want to use as shown in Figure 8.2.

As is the case with many iPad apps, the interface changes slightly if you rotate the iPad to a vertical orientation as shown in Figure 8.3.

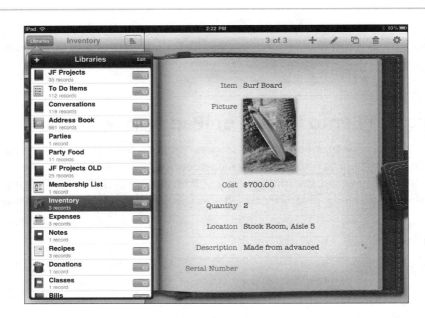

Figure 8.1   *Use the Bento iPad app horizontally.*

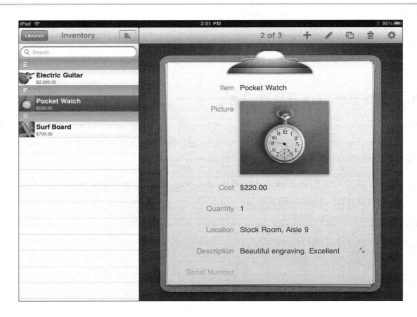

Figure 8.2   *Select a record in the Bento iPad app.*

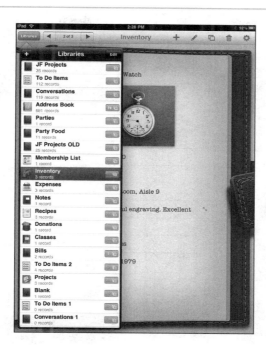

Figure 8.3   *You can use the Bento iPad app vertically.*

The toolbar at the top of the screen shows you the current record number. Tap the arrows to move forward or back; record number to show a list of the records. At the right, icons let you add a new record (the plus), modify the form and theme (the pencil), manage collections (the collections icon which is the same as in the Mac version of Bento), delete the current record (the trash can), and open Sync & Setup (the gear). To edit data within a record, just tap the field you want to change. The standard iPad interface features apply. For example, unless you have a wireless keyboard paired with your iPad, the onscreen keyboard will appear as needed. You dismiss it with the key in the lower right. To close any popover window (similar to a dialog on the Mac), just touch anywhere except on the popover.

Using the Bento App Home

The iPhone Bento app Home button shows you a view of your libraries as seen in Figure 8.4.

Switch between the two types of views with the button at the top left of the screen. In Cover Flow, when you select a library, an info button at the lower right lets you see the name and number of records in the library as well as the number of records in each of the library's collections.

Cover Flow view   List view

Figure 8.4   *Home displays your libraries in Cover Flow or a list.*

At the lower left, the edit button (a pencil) lets you edit the library's name. Tap the library name to change it. Drag the three horizontal lines at the right of each row to change the order of the libraries, and use the barred red circle at the left to delete a library. (Note that libraries such as Address book cannot be deleted here.)

On the Bento iPad app, the library editing features are enabled when you tap the Edit button at the top of the list of libraries as shown in Figures 8.1, 8.2, and 8.3.

Both the info button and the edit button are shown in Figure 8.5.

Searching the Libraries

The Search button opens the keyboard for a standard search of the data in your Bento libraries on iPhone or iPad. As you can see in Figure 8.6, the search shows records that contain the wanted text organized by the libraries in which they appear. Note that the text that has been found may not be shown in the results list because it is only visible inside a record. On iPhone, you tap Search at the bottom of the Bento screen as shown in Figures 8.4 and 8.5. On iPad, the Search box is at the top of the Libraries list as shown in Figure 8.6.

Figure 8.5   *Use the info button and the pencil button for more information.*

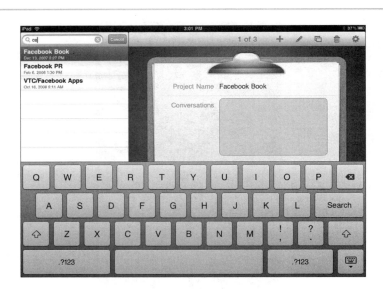

Figure 8.6 *Search libraries.*

As you will see, the same fast searching is used throughout iPhone. As you type the name, the search results are updated. With each new character, the search results are usually fewer because you have provided more detailed search information (such as an entire name rather than the first two characters).

Creating a New Library

This button lets you create a new Bento library on your iPhone. On iPad, use the + at the upper left of the Libraries list shown in Figures 8.1 and 8.3. Just as with Bento on your Mac, there are templates you can use to get started. The templates are

- Blank
- Projects
- Contacts
- To Do Items
- Recipes
- Diet Log
- Events

- Files
- Inventory
- Event Planning
- Time Billing
- Home Inventory
- Expenses
- Exercise Log

- Vehicle Maintenance
- Classes
- Digital Media
- Student List
- Membership List
- Products for Sale

- Equipment
- Issue Tracking
- Items Sold

- Customers
- Donations
- Notes

- Time Billing
- Expenses

These are similar to the templates your find in Bento on your Mac; there are a few more templates on the Mac. You will find a few changes and modifications. Remember that once you have created a library either on your iPhone, iPad, or your Mac, you can sync it so that it appears on the other device. Each template has the needed fields just as you find on your Mac. If you create a library from the Blank template, you are prompted to add the first field; you can then continue adding more fields.

To modify a library or work with related records, synchronize with your Mac and use Bento on your Mac to make the modifications as described in the chapters you have read. Added or changed fields including fields with related records will be synchronized with your iPhone or iPad.

Working with a Bento iPhone App Library

When you select a library from Home on your iPhone, you first see all of its records in a list as shown in Figure 8.7 (left). Use the + button at the upper right to add a new record or tap an existing record to edit its data as shown in Figure 8.7 (right).

The data is displayed in a standard iPhone list. For each record, one or two fields are displayed with their data. Tap any field to enter or change its data. The standard iPhone tools for typing with the keyboard, selecting dates, and entering URLs and phone numbers are available depending on the field type. You don't have to do anything: Bento and the Bento iPhone App make it all just happen as you expect.

Next to the + in the upper right that lets you add records, the standard sort button appears (it is a stack of bars of varying lengths indicating ordering). Tap it to set the sort order and to choose the primary and secondary fields to be displayed in the list.

Below the data, you find arrows to let you go to the previous and next record as well as a button to let you create a collection or add this record to an existing collection. A trash can lets you delete the record.

Figure 8.7   *View records in a library (left) or a single record (right).*

Synchronizing Libraries Between your iPhone or iPad and your Computer

Synchronization is a simple and speedy process. There are usually only two issues about which you need to be concerned: Your Mac and your iPhone or iPad must be on the same Wi-Fi network, and Bento must be running on both. Also the first time you sync you have a few extra steps that you may have to go through (they are described in "Doing Your First Sync" later in this section). For general use, however, just launch Bento on both devices and tap Sync & Setup at the bottom of the Bento for iPhone app's screen.

Understanding "Same Wi-Fi Network"

When you synchronize your Address Book or iCal data with MobileMe, the connection is over the Internet. Anywhere in the world, your Mac can synchronize with your MobileMe account and from there to other computers or an Exchange Server. You may use a Wi-Fi network to connect to the Internet, or you may be hard-wired in through an Ethernet connection (and, yes, there are still people who use dial-up connections). On the Internet, all connections are equal with the exception of their speed, and in some areas of the Internet some constraints and filtering prevent connections.

All devices attached to the Internet have an IP address. There are two versions of IP addresses: the older version (IPv4) uses a set of four numbers. These IP address may be assigned to large companies, Internet providers, and to local area networks—subnets. Two sets of addresses (192.168.x.x and 10.x.x.x) can have 65,536 and 16,777,216 nodes, respectively, on their subnets; they are reserved for such networks. They are always addressable from other areas of the Internet by going to a higher-level network, which then is subdivided. The two keys to a subnet are that any device on it can be reached in a single hop (which means you can address it directly, not by going to another subnet and finding the appropriate location) and that the subnet has a router that connects to other networks and the Internet as a whole. The router may also dynamically assign IP addresses.

Bento synchronization is limited to the subnet that you're on, so it is not Internet-wide as is MobileMe synchronization. Most of the time you do not have to worry about this. If you connect your device to your Wi-Fi network in your home, office, or school, and if your Mac is connected to the same network, all is well.

You may encounter problems in two situations. Both Airport on your Mac and your iPhone or iPad let you choose from any available Wi-Fi networks. If they are on different networks, however, you cannot synchronize your Bento data. Likewise, in a school or office, you may have a Wi-Fi network as well as access to a wired network, but if these networks are on different subnets, synchronization cannot occur.

If you have problems with synchronization, check with your technical support staff. This is not a Bento issue; it is a networking issue, so you might want to show them this page in the book. Fortunately it is usually easy to resolve, and, once resolved, you are set.

TIP

You can bypass your iPhone's network settings for a synchronization. The easiest way is to use Settings to turn Airplane Mode on. This turns off the telephone access and the network access. Then, with Airplane Mode still on, use Settings to turn Wi-Fi back on (this is directly beneath Airplane Mode). Choose the network you want to connect to and perform the sync. When you are done, turn Airplane Mode off, and you are back to your normal network settings. On iPad, there is no telephony and, thus, no Airplane Mode; you can turn Wi-Fi off with Settings.

Doing Your First Sync

The first step in syncing is to prepare Bento on your Mac and your Bento iPhone or iPad app for synchronization. You can do either one first, but you have to do both processes to begin (in other words, do not plan on setting up your Mac on Monday and your mobile device on Tuesday). This set of steps combines the mobile device and Mac setup into a logical order. It starts from your being connected to the same Wi-Fi network.

 **LET ME TRY IT**

Set Up Your First Sync

1. With Bento on your Mac, begin by choosing File > Set Up Sync with Device as shown in Figure 8.8.

2. The devices synced with Bento on your Mac are listed below the Libraries & Fields pane as shown in Figure 8.8 (the menu partially obscures the Devices section in Figure 8.8). If you already have a pairing, you will be warned with the dialog shown in Figure 8.9. You can cancel the setup right here if you have made a mistake.

3. If you proceed (or if you did not have a conflict), you will now see a list of the available devices as shown in Figure 8.10. The list may be empty at this moment.

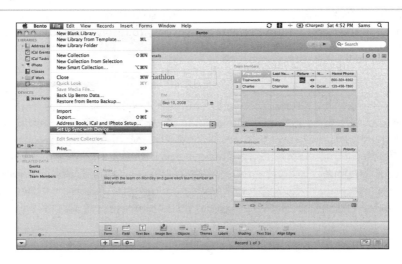

Figure 8.8 *Set up syncing from Bento on the Mac.*

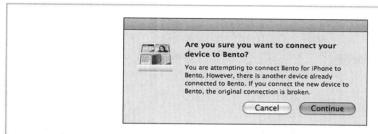

Figure 8.9   *You are warned if you already have a pairing.*

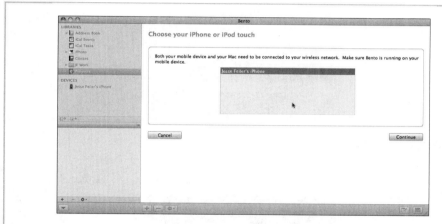

Figure 8.10   *Choose the device to pair.*

4. On the iPhone or iPad, open the Bento app and tap Sync & Setup at the lower right (iPhone) or with the gear at the right of the toolbar at the top of the screen (iPad). On the next screen, you can choose to sync over an existing pairing, or you can sync with a new computer as shown in Figure 8.11.

5. Choose to sync with a new computer. You will now see the device in the window shown previously in Figure 8.10. If the iPhone is paired with another Mac, you may be warned at this point. If you continue you will be shown four numbers on the iPhone to start the synchronization as shown in Figure 8.12.

6. Type those numbers into Bento on your Mac as shown in Figure 8.13.

Figure 8.11   *Begin the sync setup on your iPhone.*

Figure 8.12   *Use the pairing code.*

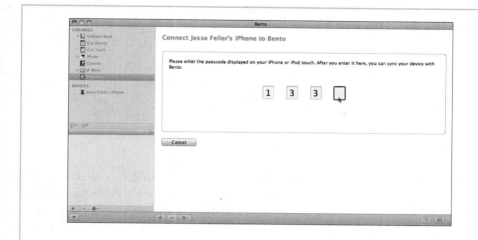

Figure 8.13 *Type the four numbers generated by your iPhone into Bento on your Mac.*

You are now set up for synchronization. By default, all of your libraries will be synced. At any time you can change these settings. On your Mac, select the device from the Libraries & Fields pane. This shows you the library synchronization options shown in Figure 8.14.

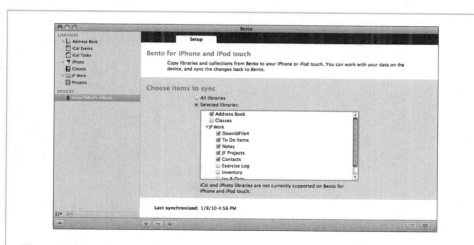

Figure 8.14 *Select the libraries you want to sync.*

TIP
If you choose not to sync everything, make certain that you make the logic very clear. Most people sync everything so that they don't have to worry about what is or isn't synced. Files bigger than 10MB are not synced, so you don't have to worry about crowding your iPhone memory.

Performing a Sync

Once your Mac and your iPhone are set up (*paired* is the term that is used), you perform a sync by tapping Sync & Setup at the bottom of the Bento iPhone app or the gear at the right of the toolbar on the Bento iPad app, and then tap Sync Now (it is shown in Figure 8.11). If you want to change the sync settings, click the device in the Fields & Panes list and select the libraries as shown previously in Figure 8.14.

Securing Your Bento Data on Your Mobile Device

If you are worried about the security of the data on your iPhone or iPad, you can set a four-character passcode lock on your iPhone. Do so by choosing Settings, General, and Passcode Lock. If you want to protect only your Bento data, tap Turn Passcode On at the top of the settings shown in Figure 8.11. This will set up a passcode for Bento only. (Setting a passcode for Bento is usually not necessary if you have a passcode for all your iPhone data.)

Sharing Data with Other Bento Users

This chapter shows you how to share your Bento data with other users on your local area network.

Beginning with Bento 3, you can share Bento libraries with other users in real time. This sharing is limited to up to five other users on your subnet, but for many people, that is more than enough. In fact, a large number of shared Bento libraries are shared among a small workgroup that may in fact consist only of one person. If you have two computers in your workspace, you can now run Bento on both of them and make updates to your schedule and other information as you go along. Alternatively, you may have a network in your home that includes your home office as well as other family members. Everyone can share the same libraries if you choose.

For more information, **see** "Understanding 'Same Wi-Fi Network'" in Chapter 8, "Synchronizing with the Bento iPhone and iPad Apps," p. 138.

The people at FileMaker have brought their decades of experience with databases to Bento so that you have the ability to control who can access the shared data in your libraries. Because sharing data can expose it to security issues, you can also encrypt it and protect it with passwords.

All of this is part of the sharing features in Bento 3.

Setting Up Sharing

The first thing to check is that you have two Macs on the same subnet. If you have a network (possibly centered on an Airport base station), you are all set. With the Airport network, you may have a shared Internet connection, but you do not need the Internet for Bento sharing; it only uses the local area network.

You need a copy of Bento for each computer that will be sharing. You can go to the Bento page (http://www.filemaker.com/bento) if you need to buy more copies; there is a 5-pack set that could be a good investment. At current pricing, you will save money buying this rather than buying separate copies. (Even for two copies, the 5-pack set is the same price as separate copies; for more than two, it is cheaper.)

Remember that you will be sharing the Bento databases, so you do not have to worry about moving anything. The databases and libraries stay where they are.

You will need to turn on sharing for each computer that will be involved in sharing (that is, the computer that will share libraries and the one that will use the shared libraries). Note that Bento sharing is unrelated to sharing that you set up in System Preferences under the Apple menu.

 **LET ME TRY IT**

Set Up Bento Sharing

1. You turn on Bento sharing from Bento > Preferences using the Sharing tab as shown in Figure 9.1.

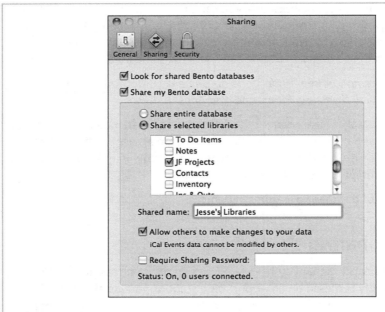

Figure 9.1 *Set up Bento sharing.*

2. Select what to share. The first two check boxes at the top of the pane let you look for shared libraries on the other computer and to share your own libraries. In many cases, a single computer is used for shared Bento libraries, perhaps the computer that is used as a file server in a small work-group. Because the Bento shared network is small (no more than five

computers), you usually know your way around it, but there are some pit-falls you might watch out for.

3. Perhaps the biggest one happens if you have libraries with the same names on two computers. This can happen very easily if you have created them from templates and not changed the names. Thus, you can easily have a Projects library on your computer, and your mother can have one on her computer, two separate libraries. They are not shared but separate. If you want to have a shared library, select one of them and use it. Renaming it (Family Projects or even Shared Family Projects) can help. This makes it easier for you. Bento uses internal safeguards to handle duplicate names properly.

4. If you click Share My Bento Database, you can either share all libraries or select specific ones to share. This is a good way to avoid confusion. Instead of sharing all of your libraries, explicitly share those you intend to share with others. That way, others will not see your Projects library, which you may want to use only for your personal (and unshared) information.

 You can further control how libraries are shared by letting or not letting people update your libraries; you can also provide a sharing password. Without it, people cannot begin to access your shared libraries. (This is separate from database passwords.) There is more on this later in this chapter under the "Using Encrypted Fields and Security" section.

The process is the same whether you are sharing your own databases or connecting to someone else's shared databases—you just check the appropriate check boxes. You can check either one, neither, or both. This means that you can simultaneously be a provider and user of shared Bento databases.

 SHOW ME   Media 9.1—A video about setting up Bento sharing
Access this video file through your registered Web Edition at
my.safaribooksonline.com/9780131388611/media.

Using Shared Libraries and Databases

Once you have set up database sharing, all you have to do is connect to the shared libraries when you want to use them. Connecting shared libraries is a fairly simple process once you have made both of them available on a network.

 **LET ME TRY IT**

Connect to Shared Libraries and Databases

1. Make certain both computers are powered on and located on the same subnet. Both need to be running the same version of Bento.

2. When shared databases are available, a Shared section appears in the Libraries & Fields pane as shown in Figure 9.2.

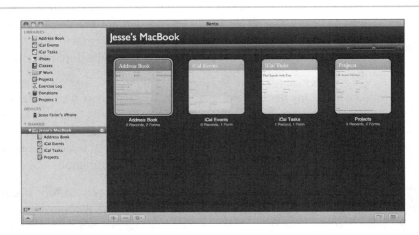

Figure 9.2 *Shared libraries appear in the Libraries & Fields pane.*

3. You see each of the shared databases, and beneath each one, you can see each of the shared libraries. You can expand or contract the databases and libraries to find which one you may want to use. (If there are no shared libraries available, the entire Shared section is not shown even if you are willing to connect to shared libraries in your Bento preferences.)

4. The small button to the right of the database name lets you log out of the database and all of its libraries. To use a shared library, click it in the Libraries & Fields pane just as you would any other library. When the database itself is highlighted, you see the libraries within it as shown in Figure 9.2.

Once you have opened a shared library, you use it almost exactly as you would a local library. The main difference is illustrated by the built-in Events library, which connects to the owner's iCal data. When shared, it can be viewed by other users, but it cannot be updated. Any field that cannot be updated has its title displayed in italics and an icon indicating no writing is shown above and to the right of the field. Futhermore, if you hover the pointer over that icon, you get a message reminding you that updating is not allowed, as shown in Figure 9.3.

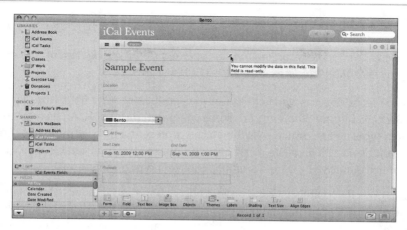

Figure 9.3 *Some fields cannot be updated when being shared (such as the Events library's fields).*

 SHOW ME   Media 9.2—A video about connecting to shared libraries and databases

Access this video file through your registered Web Edition at
my.safaribooksonline.com/9780131388611/media.

Securing Your Data

Security is usually not an issue when your databases are not shared. If you have a firewall turned on (and you should) and you do not allow screen sharing (at least without your permission), then you are reasonably safe provided that your computer is in a secure place (and if it is portable, equipped with a password and automatic log-out after a brief period of no use).

As soon as you are sharing, all bets are off. Fortunately, Bento 3 provides tools to help you keep your data secure. You can require a password for access to your database as well as a password for access to your shared data. Furthermore, you can create encrypted fields in which the data is not visible unless the database password is entered. Each of these security components has a different role to play; you can use the ones you want.

TELL ME MORE   Media 9.3—A discussion about implementing the best security

Access this audio recording through your registered Web Edition at ***my.safaribooksonline.com/9780131388611/media****.*

You can create an *encrypted* field just as you would any other field. Note that, in this, Bento is slightly different from some other database tools. An encrypted field is a field type: It can contain text, which can represent a date, a number, or anything you decide it will be. In some other database tools, you can create a specific type of field—such as a date—and just apply encryption to it.

For example, if you are sharing a project library based on the Bento template, you might want to add a confidential budget amount to the library. You will want to keep track of the budget, and you might want one other person to keep track of it, but people who are checking the progress of tasks may not need to see the budget value.

 **LET ME TRY IT**

Use Encrypted Fields

1. Create an encrypted field. Figure 9.4 shows how you can add a field called Confidential Budget to the Projects library template.

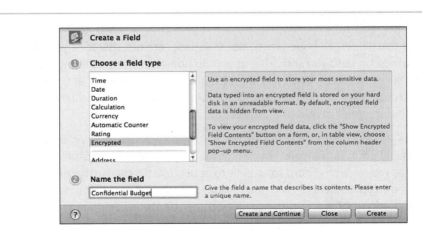

Figure 9.4   *Add a Confidential Budget encrypted field to a project library.*

2. When you type into an encrypted field, you see the text that you type.

3. As soon as you click or tab out of the field, the text is replaced by dots as is the case with passwords.

Whether or not encrypted fields are unlocked to allow viewing and changing their data is controlled by the database password and the Lock/Unlock Encrypted Fields command in the Bento menu.

 **LET ME TRY IT**

Use a Database Password

The Lock/Unlock Encrypted Fields command is in the Bento menu because it applies to all of the libraries in your Bento database. You do not have to lock or unlock individual fields or even individual libraries. (In fact you cannot do so.)

1. Set the database password from Bento Preferences using the Security tab as shown in Figure 9.5.

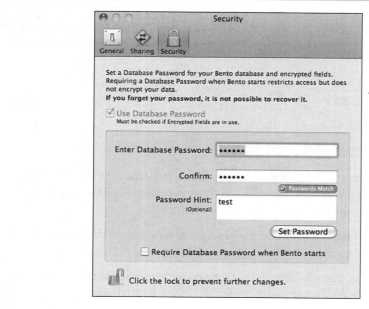

Figure 9.5 *Set a database password.*

2. Enable a database password with the checkbox at the top.

3. If you have enabled a database password, you can also require it whenever Bento is opened with the checkbox at the bottom. Remember, this is the password for the database itself: it controls access to all of your libraries, not to an individual library.

4. As you can see from Figure 9.5, this is a drop-dead password: it is stored in an encrypted format, so if you forget it, your Bento database is not accessible.

A database password is required if you have any encrypted fields in any library in your database. If you do have such fields, you cannot uncheck the box to remove the password.

If you add an encrypted field to a database that has no password, you can do so. You can even add it to a layout. But the first time you click in that field, the Security pane of Preferences shown in Figure 9.5 will open, and you will not be able to continue until you set the database password. When you close the window shown in Figure 9.5, you will no longer be positioned in the field. If you decide you do not want the encrypted field and a database password, you can delete the field.

Normally, you do provide the database password. If you have second thoughts, you can come back and delete the field. Having deleted it, you can now re-open Bento Preferences and click the Security tab. Because there is now no encrypted field in the database (unless you have created another one), you can now turn off the database password.

 **LET ME TRY IT**

Work with Locked Fields

1. Unless the entire database has been unlocked (Bento > Unlock Encrypted Fields), you are always prompted to enter the database password if you attempt to enter data in an encrypted field.

2. You can unlock the database if you required a password to open Bento (the check box at the bottom of Figure 9.5).

3. Alternatively, you can unlock all the fields in the database using the Lock/Unlock Encrypted Fields command in the Bento menu.

4. Otherwise, a click in an encrypted field prompts you to enter the password as shown in Figure 9.6.

5. After the database has been unlocked, you can view the contents of any encrypted field by clicking the view icon to its right as shown in Figure 9.7.

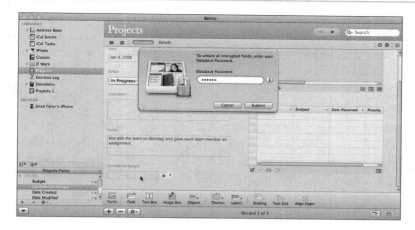

Figure 9.6 *You are prompted to enter the database password when you click in an encrypted field if the database password has not yet been entered.*

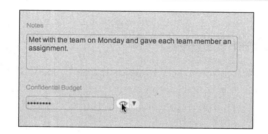

Figure 9.7 *View the contents of an encrypted field.*

6. If the database has not yet been unlocked, a padlock appears next to each encrypted field as you see in Figure 9.8.

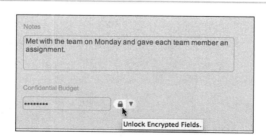

Figure 9.8 *A padlock indicates and encrypted field in an unlocked database.*

Additional commands are available at the right of this area when the database is unlocked. They let you show the contents of the encrypted field (this is the same as clicking the view icon as shown previously in Figure 9.7). You can lock all encrypted fields (this is the same as the Lock/Unlock Encrypted Fields command in the Bento menu), and you can copy an encrypted field's content to the clipboard.

TIP

If you require a password every time Bento launches, you do not have to quit Bento if you want to leave your computer for a few moments. Choose Bento > Lock Bento. The current window closes and is replaced by the password log in window shown previously in Figure 9.6. When you return to your computer, enter the password and everything will continue from where you left off.

 SHOW ME   Media 9.4—A video about working with locked fields
Access this video file through your registered Web Edition at
my.safaribooksonline.com/9780131388611/media.

Using a Sharing Password

The database password and encrypted fields protect your data on your own computer as well as when it is shared. You can add a level of security by requiring a password to open the shared database from another computer as shown previously in Figure 9.1.

With these tools, your data should be safe even when it is being shared.

Using Built-In Bento Libraries for Address Book and iPhoto

This chapter shows you how to use the Bento libraries that interact with Address Book and iPhoto

In this chapter and the two that follow, you see how to combine Bento and its tools with Address Book and iCal, applications that are built into Mac OS X. This chapter also covers Bento's integration with iPhoto, a key component of Apple's iLife suite that also contains iMovie, iWeb, iDVD, and GarageBand. Although configurations change from time to time, Apple currently pre-installs iLife on all of its computers, with the exception of the Mac mini, so a great many users of Mac OS X and Bento have iPhoto.

Bento's integration with these other programs is very tight. Address Book data is shown in a Bento library, iCal data is shown in two Bento libraries: iCal Events and iCal Tasks, and iPhoto data is shown in an iPhoto Bento library.

If for some reason you do not want Bento to use your data, you can turn off this integration; at a later time you can turn it back on. Do either task by using File > Address Book, iCal and iPhoto Setup, as shown in Figure 10.1.

Exploring the Address Book Library

You now have an Address book library in your Bento source list. Any groups that you have created in Address Book show up in the Bento library as collections in the Address Book library. Figure 10.2 shows a typical Address Book; Figure 10.3 shows that same Address Book in Bento's grid view.

You can switch back and forth between Bento and your Address Book to see how the integration works:

- If you add a record in Address Book, it shows up immediately in the Bento Address Book library. If it is added to a group, it shows up in the appropriate Bento Address Book library collection.

- If you add a record in the Bento Address Book library, it shows up in Address Book. If it is added to a collection, it shows up in the appropriate Address Book group.

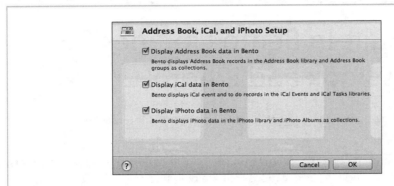

Figure 10.1   *Enable or disable Address Book integration.*

Figure 10.2   *Your Address Book data...*

- If you add a group in Address Book, it shows up in the Bento Address Book library as a collection.

- If you add a collection in the Bento Address Book library, it shows up as a group in Address Book.

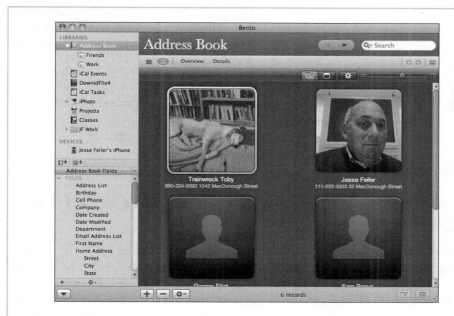

Figure 10.3   *...can show up in Bento.*

Likewise, if you delete a record, collection, or group in one place, it is deleted in the other. There is one area in which the behaviors are not linked. Smart Groups in Address Book are similar to Smart Collections in Bento. As shown in Figure 10.4, you create a Smart Group in Address Book by choosing File > New Smart Group and specifying whatever criteria you want.

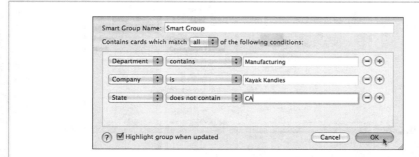

Figure 10.4   *Smart Groups in Address Book are, in some ways, like Smart Collections in Bento.*

Despite their similarities, Smart Groups in Address Book and Smart Collections in Bento are implemented in different ways, and they are not synchronized between the two applications. If you want, you can easily create a Bento Smart Collection to be the same as an Address Book Smart Group and vice versa.

 TELL ME MORE   Media 10.1—A discussion about working with **Address Book Groups and Smart Collections**
Access this audio recording through your registered Web Edition at my.safaribooksonline.com/9780131388611/media.

Extending Bento's Address Book Library with New Fields and Forms

You can add fields to the Bento Address Book library, but before you do so, make certain that the field you want to add does not already exist in Address Book. Many people do not realize that the default template in Address Book shows only some of the available fields. You can use Card > Add Field, as shown in Figure 10.5, to add any of the additional fields that simply are not shown on the template. This command adds the selected field to the given record; if you choose Edit Template, that field is added to the default template.

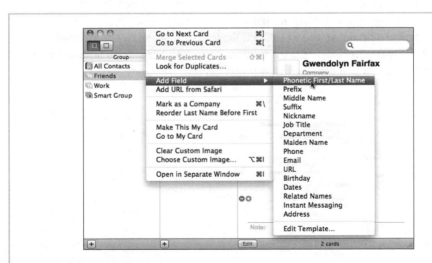

Figure 10.5   *Add Address Book fields in Address Book.*

TIP

If you attempt to enter a duplicate name through Bento, you are warned that the name already exists, and you are not able to enter it. If the name you enter is identical except for its capitalization, Bento lets you enter it. Thus, if you accidentally recapitalize an Address Book field name, you are able to create another field. If you rely on the difference in capitalization, you are leaving yourself open to confusion (your own) in the future. Use different names, and do not duplicate Address Book data.

You can modify Bento forms or create new ones using the Address Book fields. Figure 10.6 shows you the fields available in the Bento Address Book library. They map pretty clearly to the fields in Address Book.

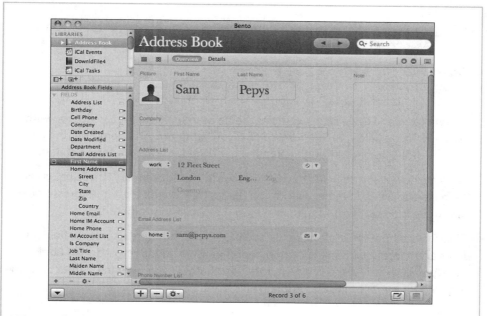

Figure 10.6   *Add Address Book fields in the Bento Address Book library.*

In Figure 10.7, you can see the fields for the table view of the Bento Address Book library and the hierarchies of fields. For example, if you click Home Address, all the fields in that address are added. As Figure 10.7 shows, you can then choose to display only some of those fields.

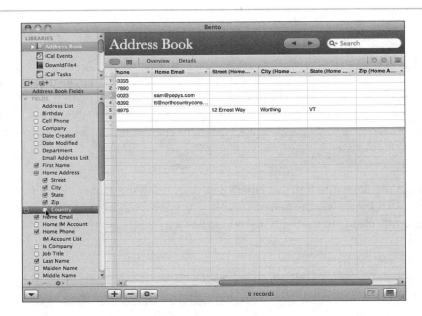

Figure 10.7   *Use field hierarchies in table view.*

In both form and table views, some of the fields in the Fields list are locked with a padlock. These fields are in Address Book; you cannot delete them from the Bento Address Book library, although you need not display them on a form or a table.

You can, however, add fields to your Bento Address Book library. These fields can then be displayed on tables or forms in Bento; they do not exist in Address Book, and there is no way to add them there, so they exist only in Bento.

Finally, note how some of the fields, such as phone numbers, use Bento field and interface constructs. There is a phone number list in your Bento Address Book library, and it is the same phone number list that you saw used in Chapter 5, "Working with Phone, URL, IM, and Address Fields and Lists in Contacts."

Synchronizing Address Book

To be precise, Address Book and the Bento Address Book library are not synchronized. Synchronizing refers to taking two separate data sources and making their contents consistent. Records may be added to one or the other or deleted from one or the other; changes within records are copied back and forth as necessary until the two data sources are the same.

That does not happen with the Bento Address Book library because, as you have seen, the data resides in Address Book and is displayed and manipulated in the Bento Address Book library even though its storage is in Address Book.

But Address Book itself can be synchronized using a MobileMe account or an iPhone. And as a result of that synchronization, the data that you see in the Bento Address Book library can change.

The common Address Book/Bento fields are synchronized. Fields that you add to the Bento library exist only in that library. They are not synchronized with or shown in Address Book.

> **NOTE**
> Most of the time, synchronization just works for you, and you do not have to worry about how it happens. The following sections provide details that you can use to understand the process or to troubleshoot problems.

Synchronizing Address Book with MobileMe

MobileMe is a subscription service from Apple that provides you with a number of features including a me.com address, disk storage on Apple's servers, and synchronization. Apple has long specialized in providing integration to its users—integration of hardware and software, integration among its applications and the operating system, and integration with the Web and through the Web to other computers. For example, with a MobileMe account, you can mount your MobileMe disk storage on your desktop and in Finder windows just by clicking iDisk.

ⓖ *For more information on MobileMe, go to www.apple.com/mobileme.*

ⓖ *For more information on synchronizing with the iPhone Bento App,* **see** *Chapter 8, "Synchronizing with the Bento iPhone App," p. 129.*

When you have a MobileMe account, you set up Address Book synchronization from System Preferences for MobileMe, as shown in Figure 10.8. (Use the System Preferences command from the Apple Menu to open this dialog.)

The settings provided here determine how the data on your computer is synchronized with your MobileMe account. In the lower right, the Advanced button opens a new window that lets you control other computers that are synchronized to the same MobileMe account (see Figure 10.9).

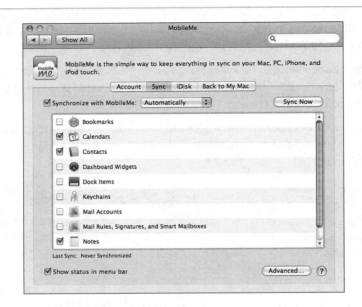

Figure 10.8   *Set up synchronization with MobileMe.*

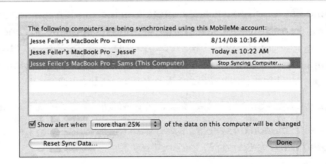

Figure 10.9   *Register the computers to be synchronized to a single MobileMe account.*

NOTE
You might think that the word "computer" does not need a definition at this point, but, in fact, it does. In the list of computers shown in Figure 10.9, notice that there are three computers with the same name (Jesse Feiler's MacBook Pro). Three separate accounts (Demo, JesseF, and Sams) are shown. The word "computer" in the world of MobileMe synchronization means a specific user on a specific computer. This means that you can share Address Book and other data

among several accounts on the same or different computers. It also means that if you want to synchronize more than one account on a computer with MobileMe, you need to supply the synchronization settings in System Preferences for each of those accounts. And, of course, the reverse situation also applies: If you have two accounts on one or more computers, they can be synchronized to two separate MobileMe accounts.

This synchronization works based on your MobileMe account name. You can have a number of computers registered to your MobileMe account; all of them can be synchronized. The process relies on MobileMe as the center of synchronization. Each computer has its own synchronization settings in its own copy of System Preferences, and each synchronizes with MobileMe according to the schedule that you set. If you do not have an Internet connection, the synchronization cannot happen. Data does not flow directly from Computer A to Computer B without going through MobileMe.

This flow of data matters because it requires at least two separate Internet connections for Computer A to be synchronized with Computer B (A to MobileMe and B to MobileMe). In practice, it often requires three connections (A to MobileMe, B to MobileMe picking up the A changes, and then A to MobileMe picking up changes from B). If you are relying on synchronization to ensure that data is consistent across several computers, remember this sequence.

In practice, unless your Address Book data is changing frequently, as long as each computer connects to MobileMe relatively often (at least once a day for most people), the data will be consistent.

Synchronization usually proceeds just as described here. However, there are cases in which you want to manually synchronize data. The Reset Sync Data button shown at the lower left corner of Figure 10.9 opens the dialog shown in Figure 10.10. You can choose to replace your local data with the MobileMe data or vice versa. Use the arrows to choose the direction of resetting. Instead of synchronizing, one data set replaces the other. You can do this for all data or specific sets of data from among the check boxes you have marked in Figure 10.8.

This approach can be a simple way to move data from one Mac to another, although if you are installing a new Mac, using a FireWire cable and the Migration Assistant inside Applications > Utilities can be easier.

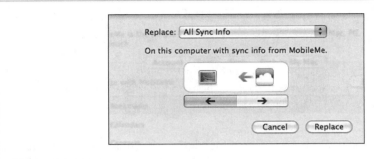

Figure 10.10 *Reset Sync Data.*

Synchronizing Address Book with iPhone

Apple has essentially perfected the synchronization process of music between a computer and an iPod and the further synchronization of music, video, address book, and calendar information between a computer and an iPhone.

> **NOTE**
> This section describes synchronization using the iPhone connected through a USB port to your computer. The following section describes the MobileMe push technology through which the iPhone and MobileMe interact directly. Chapter 8 described how to synchronize your iPhone to your computer with the iPhone Bento App. Many people use both the iPhone Bento app together with MobileMe.

As noted previously, the Bento Address Book library does not really synchronize with Address Book because it uses the Address Book data. MobileMe lets you synchronize several computers and/or accounts using the MobileMe server as an intermediary. Synchronization with iPhone is a third architecture: It is direct synchronization without the mediation of MobileMe or the Internet. You use the cord that is included with the iPhone to connect your iPhone to a USB port on your computer. After you have set up your iPhone, iTunes launches and performs the synchronization that you have specified. (You need to set up iTunes for use with your iPhone to be able to activate your iPhone; the instructions are in your getting started package.)

LET ME TRY IT

Set Up iPhone Synchronization with iTunes

1. Use iTunes > Preferences to control the backups for your iPhone, as shown in Figure 10.11.

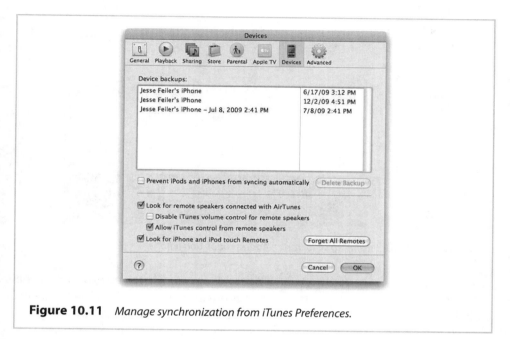

Figure 10.11 *Manage synchronization from iTunes Preferences.*

2. In the Info tab of the iPhone window that opens when you plug in your iPhone (or you can click it in the Devices list at the left), you control what specific data items are synchronized, as shown in Figure 10.12.

 SHOW ME **Media 10.2—A video about setting up iPhone synchronization with iTunes**
Access this video file through your registered Web Edition at
my.safaribooksonline.com/9780131388611/media.

The path from iPhone to your computer and thence to the Bento Address Book library is simple. If you are also using MobileMe synchronization, the path may be more complex, but it usually works without a problem. If your iPhone is paired with another computer or account, the MobileMe synchronization passes that data through to the computer on which your Bento Address Book library is located. Just remember that Bento Address Book is actually displaying and letting you edit the Address Book data on that computer and that the synchronization with other computers requires MobileMe and Internet connectivity.

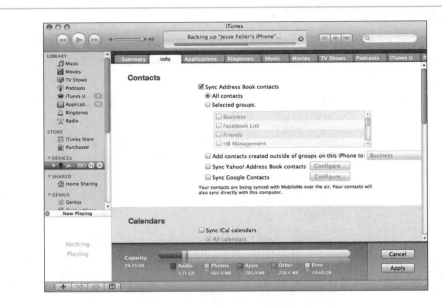

Figure 10.12 *Use iTunes to synchronize Address Book and iPhone.*

If data is not synchronized properly or does not appear where you expect it to, the easiest way to troubleshoot is to take things one step at a time. Because the Bento Address Book/Address Book connection should be the simplest, start there. Then, if you plan to synchronize your iPhone with that computer, connect it and see how the synchronization works. If there are problems, look at the Info tab, as shown in Figure 10.12, to see if you have accidentally opted not to synchronize the relevant data.

Finally, bring the MobileMe synchronization into play. Make certain that you have selected the appropriate synchronization options and that your synchronization schedule is frequent enough to pick up necessary changes.

WARNING
Before starting on synchronization, make certain that you have backed up your hard disk(s) using Time Machine or other backup software. This applies to all the computers that you may be synchronizing with MobileMe. If something goes wrong, you may wind up erasing your contacts. This usually is a result of human error (see the Reset Synchronization Data dialog shown previously in Figure 10.10; if you make the wrong choice, all is lost).

Synchronizing Address Book with PDAs and Other Devices

Other devices that store address book and contact information can often be synchronized with your Mac and thence with MobileMe, other computers, Bento Address Book, and your iPhone. They may connect with a wireless Bluetooth connection or with a cable. Apple makes the Application Programming Interface (API) to iSync and Address Book available to third parties, so they can tightly integrate their products.

The only issues you are likely to encounter have to do with slight inconsistencies in data mapping of multiple phone numbers and addresses. Usually, none of these present insurmountable hurdles.

Do be aware that synchronization is a two-way street. You will often find hardware and software that lets you import data such as address book data. An import is not a two-way transaction; it just lets you move your data from one place to another. And all too often, after your data has been stored in another device or piece of software, you cannot get it out, and you are tied into that device or software. This problem appears to be somewhat less prevalent than it was a few years ago, but before deciding to use any software that you will use to store your data, make certain that you can get out what you put in.

Using MobileMe Push Technology to Synchronize Data

Starting with iPhone OS 2.0, the iPhone can synchronize directly with MobileMe rather than with a computer. Your computer, instead, synchronizes with MobileMe over the Internet.

Because the iPhone can handle not just telephony but also Internet data, it can implement the same type of synchronization that a computer uses to synchronize over the Internet with MobileMe; it is just a matter of sending messages back and forth between the iPhone and MobileMe. If you turn Fetch New Data in iPhone Settings to Push, then the iPhone pushes new data to MobileMe as soon as the data is changed on the iPhone. There is no batch synchronization such as the process described previously. Likewise, when changes occur in MobileMe, the relevant changes are pushed down to the iPhone. This means that instead of a possibly lengthy periodic synchronization process, the process is carried out on an as-needed basis, and each process is much shorter because only one item is being synchronized at a time.

An incoming email message to your account on MobileMe is pushed down to your iPhone almost immediately. If you create an appointment on your iPhone, it shows up on your MobileMe account almost immediately. The link between computer and MobileMe, however, does still rely on the synchronization process set up in System Preferences and described in the previous section, so there may be a somewhat longer wait until the data is moved.

Finally, note that the protocols used for all this are basic Internet protocols. That is why you can synchronize Macs as well as PCs with MobileMe.

Using Mac OS X Data Detectors to Update Address Book

Data detectors are features of the Mac OS X interface that recognize certain types of data such as dates or addresses in documents and let you then work with that data in its smart form, not just as a string of text.

As you move the mouse over a data detector, a small dotted box appears around the data that has been identified. A small arrow in the lower right corner lets you bring up a contextual menu that lets you act on the data that has been detected.

If the data detector senses that it has found an address, you are given the option to add it to Address Book or to update an existing contact in Address Book. Similarly, if the dotted box surrounds a date and time, you have the option to add it to iCal.

 SHOW ME   Media 10.3—A video about using data detectors
Access this video file through your registered Web Edition at
my.safaribooksonline.com/9780131388611/media.

Now the integration of Mac OS X and Bento really shines. If you get in the habit of using the data detectors in your incoming mail, it is just a click of the mouse to add or update your Address Book directly from the Mail message as soon as you receive it. With Bento, iPhone, and MobileMe synchronization in place, that one action updates the information everywhere.

The habit of using the data detectors in Mail to update your data immediately is one that pays off not just with contact information but also with iCal information, as you will see in Chapter 11, "Using Built-In Bento Libraries for iCal Tasks and iCal Events." You can easily switch from one application to another in Mac OS X, but by using data detectors and built-in synchronization, you don't even have to do that. You need to take one action (use the data detector), and everything else is done automatically.

Exploring the iPhoto Library

If you have enabled iPhoto integration as shown previously in Figure 10.1, you will see an iPhoto library as shown in the libraries pane in Figure 10.13. (The figure shows a split view with the built-in table view at the top and the Photo Details forms below.)

Figure 10.13   *Use the iPhoto library in Bento.*

Although photos are very different from addresses, the interface is identical to that of the Address Book library. Within the iPhoto library you automatically have subli- braries for your iPhoto albums and smart albums. As you explore the iPhoto library you will see that the fields from iPhoto are locked with a padlock: you cannot remove them. However, you can add fields to your iPhoto library. Just as with fields that you add to the Address Book library, these fields and their data reside only on Bento.

Furthermore, you cannot add or remove photos or collections in the iPhoto library. These restrictions all combine to keep your iPhoto data safe while allowing you to use it in Bento.

LET ME TRY IT

Use the iPhoto Library

1. When you click the iPhoto library, you will see the albums you have created in iPhoto.

2. Select an album and view its contents in Bento's table view.

3. Compare this to Bento's grid view.

4. Use Quick Look in table view to see the image.

5. Explore the Photo Details form.

 **SHOW ME**   Media 10.4—A video about using the iPhoto library
*Access this video file through your registered Web Edition at
my.safaribooksonline.com/9780131388611/media.*

Using Built-In Bento Libraries for iCal Tasks and iCal Events

In this chapter you'll see how to use the Bento libraries to interact with iCal Tasks and Events.

Catching Up with iCal

In the preceding chapter, you saw how Address Book is integrated with Bento so that data is stored in Address Book or iPhoto but can be displayed or updated either in Address Book or iPhoto as well as in Bento. iCal is integrated with Bento in much the same way, but there are some important differences.

Perhaps the biggest difference is a reflection of the data: iCal data—like all calendaring data—is inherently more complex than address data and photos. People enter, delete, and change calendar data more frequently than address data. Even more important is the time dimension: An event scheduled for yesterday is a different type of information than one scheduled for tomorrow. The one yesterday is, and always will be, in the past. The one tomorrow changes from future to now to past as the clock relentlessly ticks. And just to make things more interesting, iCal To Dos may have dates assigned to them, but if the date passes, the To Do is still active until you mark it completed.

> **NOTE**
> This chapter focuses on iCal itself. In the next chapter, Chapter 12, "Working with Bento's Projects Library to Use Related Records from iCal Tasks, iCal Events, Apple Mail, and Address Book," you see how to bring this functionality deep into your Bento libraries.

As shown in Figure 11.1, iCal displays To Dos in a list at the right of its window. (You can show or hide the To Dos list by using a command from the iCal View menu or by using the pushpin icon in the lower right corner of all iCal windows.)

At the left of the iCal window is a Calendar list; it too can be shown or hidden with a command from the View menu. iCal events are shown in the center of the iCal window; you can switch this display from days to weeks or months. You also may see the results of a search in a pane that displays search results, as shown in Figure 11.2.

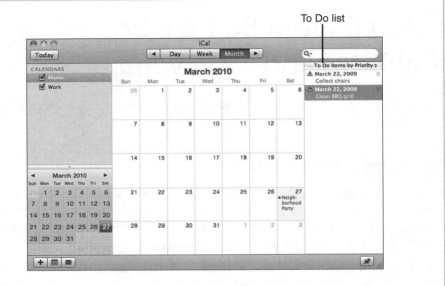

Figure 11.1   *iCal To Dos are shown at the right of the window.*

The Search Results pane appears below the calendar and To Do list, but it leaves the left-hand side of the window free for notifications, a mini-month display, and the list of calendars (you can use the View menu to show or hide any of these items).

 **LET ME TRY IT**

Search iCal

Searching for data in iCal reveals part of the underlying complexity.

1. Type a search word or phrase in the search field at the upper right of the window.

2. iCal searches for that word or phrase in To Dos as well as in events. Figure 11.2 shows both a To Do and an event with the word "clean" in them.

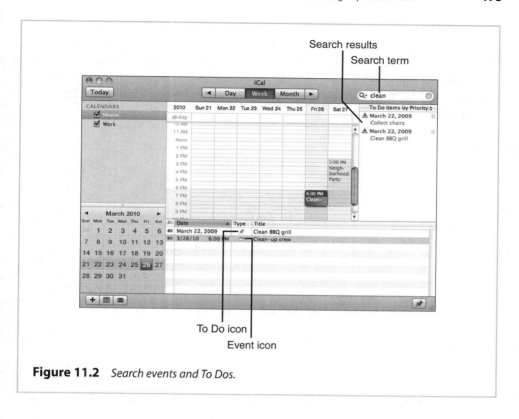

Figure 11.2 *Search events and To Dos.*

 **SHOW ME**   Media 11.1—A video about searching iCal
Access this video file through your registered Web Edition at
my.safaribooksonline.com/9780131388611/media.

Although there is an intrinsic difference between events and To Dos, there is still a great deal of commonality, as the search results show. Furthermore, many people are not aware of this, but iCal can convert one to the other. If you have an event on a calendar, you can drag it to another date or time; you can also drag its bottom or top down or up to change the start or end time. But if you drag an event to the To Dos list, instead of moving it, you copy it and automatically create a To Do based on the event. The start and stop times don't exist for a To Do, but the date of the event is preserved. Likewise, you can drag a To Do to the calendar; it is copied, and an event based on the To Do is created on the calendar.

The calendars that can organize events and To Dos are an important part of iCal. iCal begins with Home and Work calendars; you can add more if you want by clicking the plus below the Calendars list. After you have created a To Do (either just now or some time in the past), double-clicking it opens the edit window shown in Figure 11.3. You can then select the calendar with which you want the To Do to be associated.

Figure 11.3   *Edit a To Do.*

The checkboxes next to the calendars in the Calendars list determine which events and To Dos are shown.

NOTE
Calendars enable you to group events and To Dos together. They are somewhat like groups in Address Book. But there is a big distinction: A single address can be in any number of groups (including Smart Groups). An event or To Do can be in only a single calendar. One of the features of Bento's iCal libraries is the capability to organize events and To Dos so that they are in multiple Bento locations.

Because events are inherently more complex than To Dos, double-clicking an event initially opens a summary of its data, as shown in Figure 11.4.

If you click Edit, you can then edit the event, as shown in Figure 11.5.

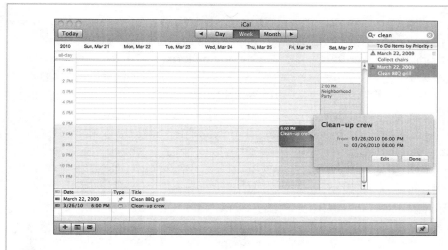

Figure 11.4   *Display event details.*

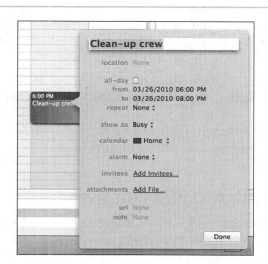

Figure 11.5   *Edit an event.*

The iCal Data Structure

iCal is built on the industry standard for Internet calendaring and scheduling ("iCalendar")—RFC 2445 from the Network Working Group of the Internet Engineering Task Force (http://tools.ietf.org/html/rfc2445). The standard was developed to allow the simple sharing of scheduling information using email and the

Web. Because this standard is open, it is supported by many products, including iCal. These products store data in whatever format they choose, but they are able to import or export that data in the common format. When such data is sent as an email attachment or embedded in a Web page, the file extension is usually .ics, and the web data type is text/calendar.

You, therefore, can use email to share iCal items or to receive them. If you make online reservations for travel or other events, you often have the option to have the reservation data sent to you. More often than not, it is sent as an .ics file; when Mail receives the file, by default it opens iCal and inserts the data there. The sender does not have to use iCal or even Mac OS X.

The standard has four main data types: events, To Dos, journals, and free time. Journal data is data associated with a date such as comments or ruminations—a journal just as in the noncomputer world. Free time is just that—time that is not taken up by an event. Currently, not many applications use the journal data. Free time is used in scheduling software. In fact, iCal supports the capability to create events and to invite people via email. It also manages incoming invitations and can automatically create events from them. The Bento libraries support only events and To Dos.

 TELL ME MORE   **Media 11.2—A discussion about the iCal data structure**
Access this audio recording through your registered Web Edition at my.safaribooksonline.com/9780131388611/media.

Exploring the Bento iCal Libraries

As you have seen, events and To Dos are related but different in their interface elements and data. Bento handles this issue by providing you with two built-in libraries: one for iCal events and the other for iCal To Dos. If you allow iCal integration using File > Address Book and iCal Integration, as described in the preceding chapter, iCal Events and iCal Tasks are added to your Source list. The data from iCal is displayed in those libraries and stored in iCal.

NOTE
iCal To Dos are Bento tasks. The only difference is the name.

One behind-the-scenes action takes place when you begin to edit iCal data in a Bento library: A new calendar is automatically added to iCal. iCal uses this new calendar, named Bento, for events and tasks that are created by Bento. You can, however, specify another calendar by changing the Calendar field's entry in the Bento library, as shown in Figure 11.6.

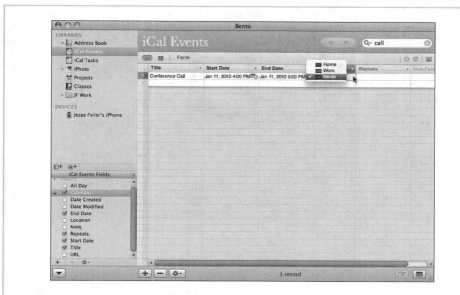

Figure 11.6   *Use iCal event data in Bento's iCal Events library.*

As you would expect, all the Bento interface tools such as date and time entry are available for editing your iCal data. Figure 11.7 shows the tool you use to edit an iCal event time in Bento. It is the same element you use for editing any date field that includes a time. Note the standard Bento date/time icon in the Start Date and End Date fields in the selected row. The data itself is shown in a row of table view that is not selected, but the selected row is ready for editing with those icons displayed.

In the Fields pane, you see that some of the fields have a padlock next to them. These are the iCal fields; they are stored in iCal and updated through iCal or Bento. You can remove these fields from a given table view or form, but you cannot remove them from the iCal database. You can add new fields in Bento; however, they are not stored in iCal. When you look at your Bento library, the presence or absence of the padlock shows you which fields can be deleted, which also shows you where the data is actually stored and, more important, whether it is visible in iCal. (Bento-only data is not visible in iCal, but everything is visible in Bento.) This behavior is identical to the behavior described in the previous chapter for Address Book and iPhoto.

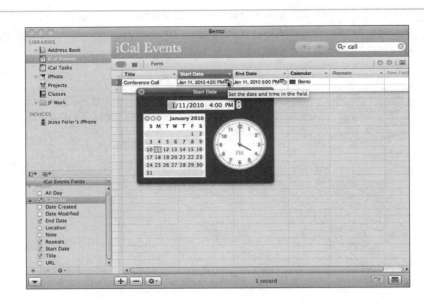

Figure 11.7   *Use Bento to edit iCal dates and times.*

The padlock appears only when you select a field in the Fields list. If no field is selected, no padlock is shown until you select a locked field that is actually stored in iCal.

Using Mail's Data Detectors with iCal

Mail's data detectors work just as well with iCal as with Address Book.

G *For information on using data detectors with Address Book, see the section "Using Mac OS X Data Detectors to Update Address Book" in Chapter 10, "Using Built-In Bento Libraries for Address Book and iPhoto," p. 168.*

LET ME TRY IT

Use Mail's Data Detectors with iCal

1. Hover your mouse pointer over a potential date in an email message to bring up a dotted box and arrow just as for addresses.

2. Click the arrow so that Mail can decode it.

3. Choose to view it in iCal or to create a new event.

Mail, together with iCal, recognizes dates such as 4/24 and assumes the current year. For a day of the week, it assumes the next occurrence—Monday means next Monday, not last Monday—and "today" means today.

TIP

If you highlight part of the email message before using the data detector, the highlighted text appears in the Notes field of the event. This capability is useful for a wide variety of data, ranging from reservation confirmation numbers to agendas for meetings that are shown in the email message.

Many people seem to live on email today. For anyone who has played telephone tag trying to schedule something, the asynchronous messaging of email is a welcome relief. You can use data detectors to quickly show a date (and time) in iCal so that you can easily see if a proposed date is free.

 SHOW ME   Media 11.3—A video about using Mail's data detectors with iCal

Access this video file through your registered Web Edition at
my.safaribooksonline.com/9780131388611/media.

The integration with iCal and Address Book means that you can frequently read an email message and handle it then and there; you don't have to remember to put it in your calendar or date book later in a second step. Not only can it save time, but also creating the iCal appointment immediately means that you don't have partially scheduled appointments floating in limbo around email messages rather than being stored in iCal.

TIP

Over the years, Apple has developed an enormous amount of software and worked on many user interface designs. Not all the development efforts have seen the light of day. Some of them that did see the light of day did not catch on. Apple has worked on the general concept of data detectors for some time. In fact, the Newton handheld device implemented some of this technology.

The Newton's implementation went a step further so that "lunch" or "dinner" could be mapped automatically to a specific time. Apple shipped that code on the Newton, and perhaps it will reappear in the Mail/iCal link. Long-time Apple watchers know that one of the best ways of seeing what Apple will be releasing in the future is to watch for places where technology from past projects can be reused.

Managing Your Calendar Data

In Chapter 12, you will see how to use Bento to bring relevant data into Bento libraries. You may be chomping at the bit to get started, but to get the most out of iCal and Bento, take a moment to think about your calendar data and how you manage it.

Managing a calendar is a personal matter. There is no right way or wrong way to do it as long as you show up on time and manage to more or less accomplish the tasks you have to perform. Although there is no right or wrong way to manage your calendar, the fact is that there are two things that can make it more likely you will miss appointments and forget about tasks. Fortunately, iCal and Bento together can address both of these issues if you do your part:

- The first way in which you can make a mess of your calendar is to try to do too much. There are only 24 hours in a day, and if you schedule 30 hours, you won't get everything done. Even if you do not account for too many hours, if you schedule two appointments at the same time, you are in trouble. For many people, the problem arises with the tasks, not with their appointments. An appointment that is in the past is over and done with regardless of whether you attended. But a To Do item just sits there and rolls over to the next day until it is done. If you are behind in those tasks, you can easily accumulate quite a handful of undone tasks that together account for perhaps a week's worth of work.

- The second common way to make a mess of your calendar is to have too many calendars. Not too many in the sense of iCal calendars, but too many in the sense of iCal and other programs, wall calendars, PDA calendars, calendars on shared websites, or traditional paper calendars. That makes it remarkably easy to schedule conflicts. In addition, if you have two hours' worth of tasks for today on one calendar, another two hours' worth of tasks on another, before long you may find yourself with more than a day's worth of tasks.

The more you rely on a single calendar to organize your life, the less likely you are to run into the problems described here. iCal lets you share data with other people by publishing calendars to the Web. In addition, if you use iCal invitations, your friends and colleagues can automatically update their calendaring software with the events that you schedule, and, presumably, they will send you invitations that iCal can manage as its own events.

Accumulating multiple calendars is remarkably easy. You may have a schedule for a sports league and a separate schedule for campground reservations. Many organizations rely on free calendaring software on their websites. This proliferation of calendars means that you have to remember to check all of them to find out when you are free or busy.

The best solution is to have a single calendar—iCal. The second-best solution is to move appointments from other calendars into iCal as soon as you find out about them. If someone has a Web-based calendar that you need to refer to, make certain that you can export events from it in .ics format. Because this is an open standard, you are asking for the export capability to be available to anyone with modern calendaring software—scarcely an unreasonable request.

TIP

There is one exception to the single-calendar suggestion. If you have a block of time that is scheduled by other people (think of your job, for example), your calendar can just account for the time as a whole. Your work appointments can live separately in their own calendar, which may even be part of a corporate database. The more your work and personal calendars are integrated (flex-time, perhaps, or colleagues from work who are also personal friends), the more you should consider having only one scheduling tool.

The issue of accumulating incomplete tasks is one that you have to address head-on. Make it a point to look at your calendar regularly (once a day for many people) and adjust your incomplete tasks. Do not just roll them over to tomorrow; instead, realistically distribute them in a reasonable schedule until they are done. And if some of them are not going to be done, face the music and delete them—or delegate them if that is a possibility. But be realistic. No matter how good you have been, the chance of your dog cleaning out the attic is probably about the same as the chance of your doing it yourself if you have not done it so far. Be creative: move.

This regular review of your schedule is actually more important when you use Bento. As you will see in the following chapter, you can integrate iCal events and tasks with project management in Bento. You can lay out events and tasks for each project in their own contexts and then view them on an iCal calendar. The project-based scheduling lets you look at things from that project's viewpoint, but you may wind up with an unbalanced schedule. Fortunately, if you overbook a day while updating projects, you can go into iCal, quickly see the conflicts (as shown in Figure 11.8), and change them there. The Bento data reflects the iCal data, so you have to make the change only once. (This technique works for events, but iCal cannot show if you have too many tasks on a given day.)

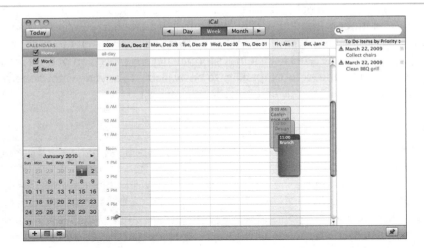

Figure 11.8   *iCal makes it easy to spot scheduling conflicts.*

Synchronizing iCal Events

The same process that is used to synchronize Address Book and other data can be used to synchronize iCal events. This is not just a matter of copying data from one place to another. From the standpoint of Bento, this is the process by which your personal information in Bento libraries on your own Mac moves out into the world of other devices. If you are using MobileMe, that information goes into the MobileMe cloud where it can be pushed or pulled to your iPhone, to PCs and Macs, and to any other device registered to your MobileMe account. Those devices, in turn, may also pass the information along to devices with which they synchronize. And, of course, the reverse is true: MobileMe, through its synchronization, brings information from the outside world—other Macs you own, PCs running Outlook, PDAs, and more to your iCal events.

 SHOW ME   Media 11.4—A video about synchronizing iCal events
Access this video file through your registered Web Edition at
my.safaribooksonline.com/9780131388611/media.

© *Apple's MobileMe service can synchronize iCal events just as easily as Address Book (and more).* **See** *Chapter 8, "Synchronizing with the Bento iPhone and iPad Apps," p. 129.*

© *For information about how to add references to your iCal events to your Bento libraries,* **see** *Chapter 12, "Working with Bento's Projects Library to Use Related Records from iCal Tasks, iCal Events, Apple Mail, and Address Book," p. 183.*

Working with Bento's Projects Library to Use Related Records from iCal Tasks, iCal Events, Apple Mail, and Address Book

Bring together related records from iCal, Address, Book, and Mail.

Exploring Projects

Bento's built-in Projects library integrates Address Book, iCal Tasks and Events, and Bento itself to provide you with a way of managing projects. The integration of the other libraries gives you a powerful way of using the data that you already have. The overall structure of the Projects library provides a way for you to keep track of the projects with which you are involved.

 TELL ME MORE   Media 12.1—A discussion about getting the most out of data integration

Access this audio recording through your registered Web Edition at
my.safaribooksonline.com/9780131388611/media.

As you move into the final chapters in this book, you'll find repeatedly that the challenges in setting up Bento libraries do not have much to do with technology: Bento has got that down cold, making databases easier than ever before for you to use. The challenges that you'll find are almost existential: How do you want to organize your life and your data? You will find suggestions from Bento and in the later chapters of this book, but ultimately you will have to decide how you want to do things.

G *In Chapter 13, "Designing a Projects Library to Share on Your LAN and Synchronize with Your iPhone," p. 195, you see how to expand the Projects library to make it an effective tool for a small workgroup.*

When you first create a library using the Projects template, you see the window shown in Figure 12.1.

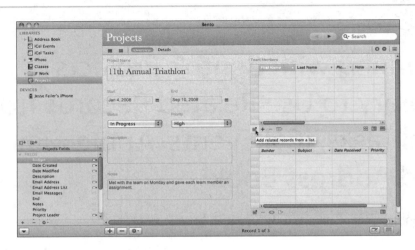

Figure 12.1   *Create a Projects library from the template.*

Several aspects of this library are different from the ones you have seen before. First, notice that two forms are provided: Overview and Details. Next, look at the bottom center of the window. There you can see that instead of one sample record as in the other templates you have seen so far, there are three so that you can get more of a sense of the template's possibilities.

In the Overview form, the Team Members field at the right is a list of related records. The highlighted icon lets you add records from the related table. In this case, as you see in the next section, it is your Address Book.

Explore the Details layout shown in Figure 12.2. Flip back and forth between the layouts to see some good Bento design techniques.

 SHOW ME   **Media 12.2—A video about creating a good Bento form design**
Access this video file through your registered Web Edition at
my.safaribooksonline.com/9780131388611/media.

Both forms contain the basic information about the project. Overview has fewer details, but it adds the description. Note that both forms leave the basic information about the project in the same location. If you design a series of forms based on the same database, decide what items you want to preserve on all the forms and then place them in the same location. You may choose to vary this information so that certain items appear on all forms and other items appear only on some forms. But to the extent that you can place the same item in the same place on each form, you will find it easier to work with the forms.

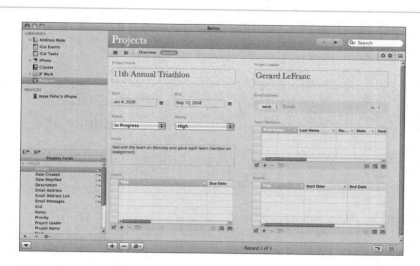

Figure 12.2 *The Details form provides greater detail.*

While you are considering your form's layout, you can take advantage of a new feature of Bento 3: image boxes. An image box can contain an image for your form. This is not an image for each record in the form (such as a photo of a product or of a person); instead, it is an image that is part of the form and that remains the same on all records.

 **LET ME TRY IT**

Add an Image to Your Form with a Image Box

1. Using the form tools at the bottom of a form or with Insert > Image Box, place an image box in the form.

2. Move and resize the image box as you see in Figure 12.3.

3. Drop an image, such as a logo, into the image box, and you now have a customized and distinctive form. You can also insert a text box either with

instructions for the form or your company name, but as you see in
Figure 12.4, many logos already contain text.

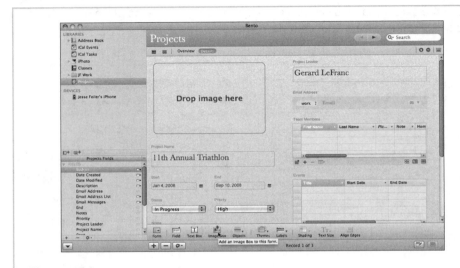

Figure 12.3 *Add an image box.*

Figure 12.4 *Add an image or logo to your image box.*

SHOW ME   Media 12.3—A video about adding an image to your form with an image box

Working with Related Records from iCal and Address Book

The Details form shows the related records from Address Book (Team Members), as well as iCal Tasks and Events.

 LET ME TRY IT

Adding Related Records

1. To add data from a list of related records, click the icon at the lower left of a related records field. (It is highlighted in Figure 12.1.)

2. Select the record(s) you want to use (see Figure 12.5). You can double-click or Shift-click to select several records.

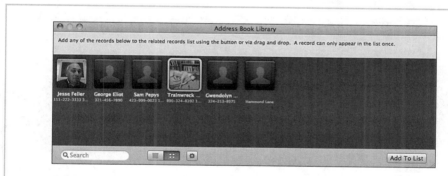

Figure 12.5   *Search for records to relate.*

3. You can also use the search field at the bottom of the dialog to search for records.

4. After you've selected the records you want, click the Add To List button. As you see from the icons listed at the bottom of Figure 12.5, you can display the records in a table view or a grid view.

TIP
A record can appear in a related records list only once. If you search for records in the related database and the Add To List button is not active, the reason is that the record has already been added. If you select several records, one or more of which have already been added to the related records list, clicking the Add To List button adds the new one and ignores the duplicates.

5. The fields you select to be shown in the related records are shown in the search dialog, as shown in Figure 12.5. However, you can search on any field that exists in the related database.

6. Use the icon in the lower right of any related records list to change the Fields pane to the related records rather than the records in the main library as shown in Figure 12.6.

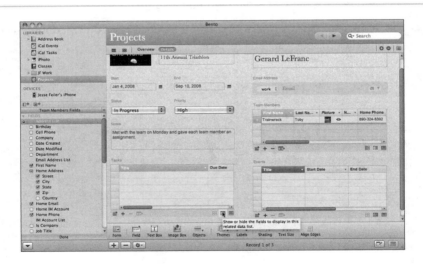

Figure 12.6   *Select fields for the related record.*

An example is using an iCal calendar that identifies the project. If you have such a calendar, you can search on its contents to find all records in iCal for calendar Project X, for example. You can then select them all and add them to the list of related records in Bento with a single click. But there is no point in showing the calendar name in your Bento list of related records; it is the same for every record in your list (Project X). Because Bento searches in all fields, you can search on Project X, select the records, and then continue on your way.

After you have established the link, the affected records are shown in the list of related records in Bento at all times. Remember that this is not a Smart Collection: If the search criterion is no longer valid, the record remains in the list of related records until you manually remove it. As is the case with all related records, if you create a new record in the list, it is stored in Address Book and related back to your Bento database.

For example, you can type into the Team Members related records list in the Projects library to add a new team member, as shown in Figure 12.7. Click the + at the lower left of the related data field to begin entering the new team member's data.

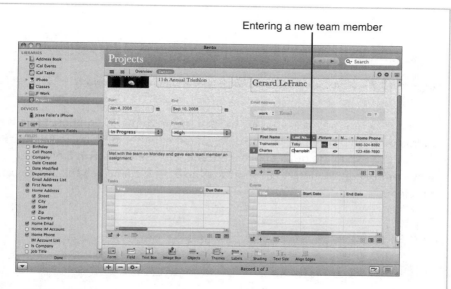

Figure 12.7 *Add a new team member in the related records list in the Projects library.*

When you go to Address Book, that person is now included in the Address Book without doing anything else, as shown in Figure 12.8. Furthermore, if you type a note into the Address Book record, it immediately appears in the Notes column of the Team Members field in Projects.

If you are filling a project with data from iCal and Address Book, you will probably use the search technique frequently. On the other hand, if you are starting a new project from scratch, you may do your data entry in Bento and rely on its being updated externally. Of course, you may choose both: Your project members may already be in your Address Book, but the tasks you create may be more logically created in Bento.

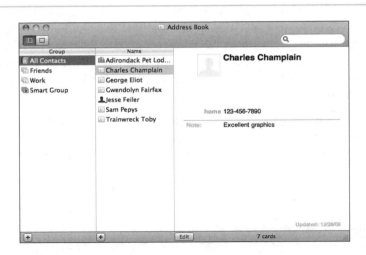

Figure 12.8   *Data is automatically shared from Address Book to Projects.*

Although Bento can make your life much easier with this integration, there is one point you should bear in mind: he data you enter either in Bento, in Address Book, or iCal is shown in the other application, and it is often shown in a different context—or none at all. Figure 12.9 illustrates an example in which this can cause a problem.

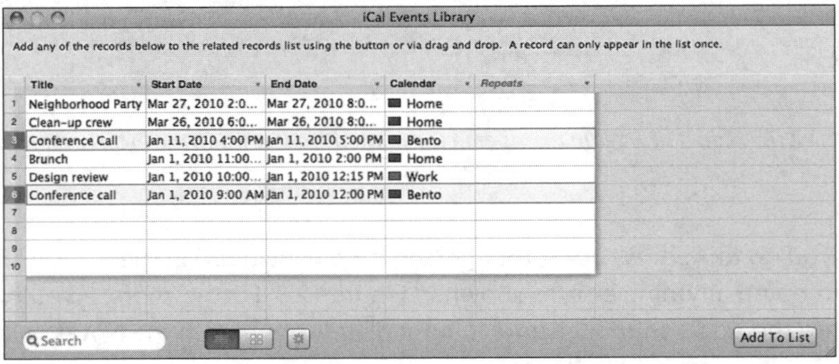

Figure 12.9   *Avoid ambiguous event and task names.*

If you were importing data into a Bento project, would you choose to import an event labeled simply as "Conference Call"? What conference call? You can use iCal calendars to organize your data there, and you can see the calendar data in Bento, but that may not be enough.

Here are some of the ways you can prevent confusion. Use any or all of them (or others) that make sense to you. Remember that confusion can go in both directions. If you add an event called "Meeting" to the related records list for a project, it is very clear what that event is so long as you are in Bento. When you look at that event in iCal, it is a big mystery. To address this issue you can do one of the following:

- Create an iCal calendar for each of your Bento projects and assign the appropriate tasks to it. Then you can use the Bento search to quickly find new records to be added. Do this whenever you think there might be new records. As noted previously, Bento makes certain that you do not add related records twice.

- If there is likely to be any ambiguity, use an abbreviation for the project in the name, such as "ABCProj: conf. call." Just make certain you use the same abbreviation everywhere else. (You can also place this in the notes or other field for the item.)

- Make certain the event name is unambiguous. This means it should clearly identify the project, and it involves more typing than the two preceding methods.

 SHOW ME   Media 12.4—A video about adding related records
Access this video file through your registered Web Edition at
my.safaribooksonline.com/9780131388611/media.

Working with Related Records from Mail

Bento's Mail integration is slightly different in its interface from the iCal and Address Book interfaces. There, and in other related records list fields, you can search for data to add to the related records list, as shown previously in Figure 12.6. In a related list of email messages, that icon opens Mail itself. You use Mail's searching and organizing tools to select the messages you want to relate.

As Figure 12.10 shows, you can choose messages or other messages such as RSS feed messages from Mail. When you click the Choose Apple Mail Items icon shown in Figure 12.10, Mail opens so that you can select and drag the messages you want into the Bento field. Any type of Mail message can be used in Bento: If it is in Mail, you can add it to a Bento email message list.

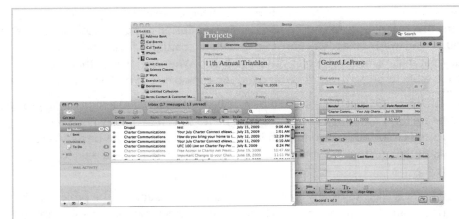

Figure 12.10   *Add messages to Bento.*

Customizing Fields and Revising Forms

As noted previously, people have their own ways of organizing calendar data. In addition, different projects sometimes require different tools and techniques. The changes that you make in the Projects library itself have to serve for all the projects that you will use. Fortunately, Bento is so easy to modify (and remodify and unmodify) that you do not have to worry.

One of the simplest customizations to make is to remove the fields that you do not need from the forms. Also, if you use different terminology, feel free to rename the fields. Remember that Bento is your personal database, so make certain that your user—you—is satisfied.

> **NOTE**
> Initially, remove the fields from the forms, not from the database. Then, when you are satisfied that you really do not need them, you can remove them from the database. Remember that once a field is removed from the database, its data is gone. Cleaning up is good, but wait to do your cleaning until you are satisfied with your changes.

As you work with the Projects library, you may find that you want different ways of looking at the data. Remember that you cannot only modify forms but also create new ones. Make the data as clear as you can. Often that means creating extra forms to display the project data in different ways. If you have two or three types of projects (such as projects you work on by yourself, volunteer projects, and projects at work), you may want to see the data in different ways for each type of project.

Creating and Sharing Calendar Events and Address Book Contacts with MobileMe

iCal and Address Book both can synchronize with other computers, iPhones and other devices, and MobileMe. You can use the MobileMe synchronization to share events and contacts with other people.

MobileMe is much more powerful than the Mac environment that preceded it (in part because of advances in Web technology). It winds up doing two different but related things:

- It keeps all your devices synchronized with almost no effort on your part; your data is the same on all of them.

- It allows you to synchronize some or all of your data with other people on Macs or PCs. In this way, it is a bridge from the private world of your Mac (or Macs) and your iPhone or PDA to other people.

The first step is to create a MobileMe account if you do not have one. To do so, go to http://www.mobileme.com.

If you want to synchronize your data with another Mac of yours (perhaps home or office), the setup for that Mac is basically the same. In fact, synchronizing with a PC running Outlook on Windows is the same basic process.

The integration that MobileMe makes possible is important, but Bento takes it even further. Entering a new team member in the related records list for a project in Bento can update Address Book and, through MobileMe, the Address Book data on the Web. Furthermore, although you don't see it, that data has now been updated on your iPhone and perhaps other computers.

Whether it is a contact, an event, or a task, most people think about entering the data when they are working with it—for example, when they are working on the particular project that contact, event, or task is associated with. In the bad old days (before Bento), you had to switch from what you really wanted to do (manage the project) to update your address book or calendar. Now, all that maintenance is done for you automatically through Bento, MobileMe, and the Mac OS X applications.

CAUTION

There is one thing to watch out for. If you add a contact, event, or task through a Bento-related records list, the appropriate data source (Address Book or iCal) is updated with the new record. If the contact, event, or task already exists, you wind up with duplicate entries. In most cases, this is not a major problem because you probably know, in general, who is in your Address Book and what is likely to be in iCal. For example, if you add someone you know to a Bento project, that person is likely to be in your Address Book. If it is someone new and you are copying information from a business card you have just been given, chances are the person is not in your Address Book. If there is any possibility, search for the person, task, or event as described previously in this chapter.

13

Designing a Projects Library to Share on Your LAN and Synchronize with Your iPhone

Find how to share a projects library over your LAN and on your iPhone.

Taking Another Approach to Projects

In the previous chapter, you saw how to integrate Bento's libraries that access Address Book as well as iCal Tasks and Events. Together with a MobileMe account, this can mean that from your Bento Projects library you can add and modify the data, which then can be synchronized with other Macs and your iPhone. Beginning with Mac OS X 10.6 (Snow Leopard), you can also synchronize data with a Microsoft Exchange server. This means that you can see all of your data in one place no matter whether it resides on your Mac, the Microsoft Exchange Server, or your iPhone. If you are sharing your Bento libraries over a LAN, you can share their data as well as your Address Book and iCal data.

There are some issues involved in sharing data from these external sources; for many people they do not matter and never arise. Nevertheless, you should be aware of these issues. For example if you share your iCal events through the Bento Events library, it cannot be edited by others.

One very common case of sharing and synchronization occurs if you have an iPhone that is synchronized with a Bento library that resides on your main computer (for many people today, this can be a MacBook that is almost always with them—though not quite so much as an iPhone, which is absolutely always with them). In addition, you may have another Mac in an office, den, or other location that you frequently use. This could be another MacBook, but it also could be an iMac, Mac mini, or Mac Pro. You may even have a variety of other Macs that you frequently use and that also participate in sharing. When Bento is running on the various computers of the same LAN, the libraries can be shared, but remember that the sharing is always *from* a computer on the network to up to five other computers on the network. A given computer can be on both sides of the sharing paradigm, but a given library is always hosted on a single computer.

In this scenario, your MacBook may have your Bento libraries on it, and when you are within range of the other computers on the same LAN, they can connect to that shared library. If you and your MacBook go off to a camp in the Adirondacks where you may have a solar-powered recharger for your MacBook but no other modern technology, you can update information in your Bento library, but even though you marked that library as sharable it will not actually be shared by any other computers (unless you've brought your friends and their MacBooks along to the campsite).

When you return to your home, school, or office and are once again within range of the other computers, your library with your new information can be shared by them, and they can update your library. This may be exactly what you want, but you may want to be able to go off with your MacBook while still allowing your office to function with the shared library.

In that case, you want the shared library to be placed on one of the computers that is in the office and, often, a computer that is always on. You can use such a system's Energy Saver control panel to allow it to sleep with very little power consumption; just make certain to enable the Wake for Ethernet Network Access check box as shown in Figure 13.1.

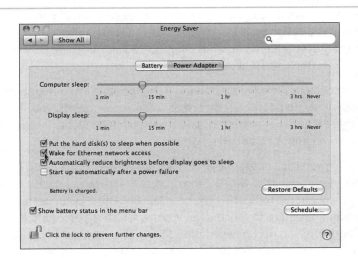

Figure 13.1 *Allow an always-on computer to sleep and wake as needed.*

This setup lets you have an always-on computer in your shared workspace so that anyone (including you) can access it when they are on that LAN and have Bento running on their Macs. Anyone who leaves the LAN no longer has access to the shared library.

One person, however, can synchronize the shared library with an iPhone. Remember that an iPhone can only be synchronized with one computer, and one computer can be synchronized with only one iPhone. In addition, one iPad can be synchronized with that computer. It works just as a synchronized iPhone does. These can be changed, but the configuration is designed for relatively stable synchronizations not those that change by the minute. Because of this synchronization option, if you are the owner or main user of the shared library that resides on the always-on computer back in the office, you can take your iPhone with the synchronized library with you when you go off to the campsite or any other location. When you and your iPhone are back on the same LAN as the shared library, you can synchronize the iPhone and the shared library so that the same data is on both. Any users who are using the shared library will also see that updated data (see Figure 13.2). Thus, there are in effect two versions of the shared library—but it is only two (Mac and iPhone) and no more.

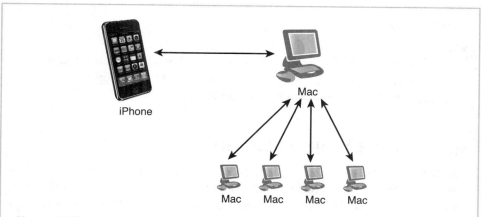

iPhone

Mac

Mac   Mac   Mac   Mac

Figure 13.2 *An iPhone can share a Bento library with one Mac. That Mac can share a library with up to four other Macs on a local network.*

The key to this is the one-to-one synchronization between the shared library and a single iPhone as well as the ability for up to four other computers to connect to the shared library. If you want an environment in which anyone who uses the database can make changes at any time from anywhere without the restriction of being on the same LAN, you need a different type of software. Fortunately it exists: Use FileMaker Pro of FileMaker Server to host the database (you can import it into

FileMaker from Bento). FileMaker Pro and FileMaker Server are designed to handle this situation. With FileMaker Pro you still are limited to five users, but they need not be on the same LAN: They can be on any networks that can communicate with one another (even if they use the Internet and are halfway around the world from one another). With FileMaker Server, the limit for the number of simultaneous users is well up into the hundreds.

You may want to expand the Bento Projects library to include additional data that can be shared in these ways. You also may want to deliberately not use your iCal and Address Book data. The most frequent example of this is when you want to keep your event, task, and contact information together with your project data and not in your Address Book or iCal. You may have set up synchronization with iCal and Address Book so that your data is widely available through MobileMe, which may not be what you want for a certain project's data. Of course, one way to handle this if a separate always-on computer in your office is set up with iCal and Address book and you don't synchronize them with your own data. In fact, a separate MobileMe account might be just what you want to have the advantages of automatic synchronization without the potential problems of sharing data that should not be shared.

Fortunately Bento and Mac OS X let you set up sharing and synchronization in whatever way works for you.

 TELL ME MORE   Media 13.1—A discussion about related records
Access this audio recording through your registered Web Edition at
my.safaribooksonline.com/9780131388611/media.

Exploring the Projects Library

The basic Projects template lets you describe the project, add notes, and associate information from Address Book (team members) and iCal (tasks and events). You can also add messages from Mail. Figure 13.3 shows the Projects library before any changes have been made.

Regardless of which Bento version you are using, you can rearrange this template's various elements as you see fit. Perhaps, for example, you tend to work with larger or smaller teams: You can change the size of the Team Members related list field to reflect that.

As you can see in Figure 13.2, a Notes field is included in the library. As you start to explore the library, you may discover what may be a limitation for you.

The sample data in Figure 13.2 shows the project lasting over a period of eight months. The note says, "Met with the team on Monday and gave each team member an assignment." Which Monday? How many such notes might accumulate in this Notes field over the course of the project? How will you find the new ones, let alone deal with old ones?

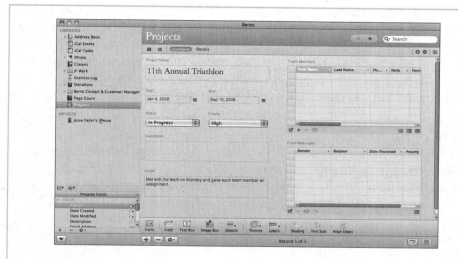

Figure 13.3 *Start from the Projects library.*

iCal manages tasks and events—things that happen in the future. You can look at events from the past as well as completed tasks, but the emphasis in any calendar is on the future.

One aspect of project management for many people is keeping track of what has happened in the past—items such as the sample note in Figure 13.3. Because iCal and the Bento Projects library handle tasks and events, if you want to organize and structure your notes, you have to do so yourself. In this chapter, you see how to construct a table for notes that you can relate to a modified version of the Projects library.

Organizing and Implementing Notes: The Basics

The whole point of using a database is to organize your data so that you can easily retrieve it as you need it. Bento makes it easy not only to structure the data but also to modify the structure as well as the data. One way to go about creating a Notes table to be related to Projects is simply to create a table with a single field— Note—and relate it. This section shows you how to do that. You can then modify the Notes table to add additional fields and to structure it a bit more. The following section shows you how to do that.

Remember that by implementing notes as a related table, you are able to use all the relational tools that Bento supports, including the display of records in a scrolling list, the summary row at the bottom, and the like. The related table can be synchronized with an iPhone and shared just as your other Bento libraries are. You will see that on the iPhone Bento app, you can view the records from the related library, and you can view the related records in your main project record. However, the iPhone Bento app does not support the creation of related records. This means that notes have to be entered on Bento running on a Mac. Once you have synchronized with the iPhone, the notes will be there, and you can even modify or delete those records, but you cannot create new related ones.

> **NOTE**
> For most people, creating a Bento library is an iterative process. Remember: you are the user. You can do what you want. In general, it is a good idea not to remove fields from the database unless you are certain that the data they contain appears elsewhere or doesn't matter. (It is easy to forget that a field not required for the current record in a database may matter very much for other records.) If you find yourself modifying your libraries and database a great deal, consider the tips later in this chapter in the section "Enhancing the Relationship."

The steps involved in creating the related table are

- Create a new Bento library for notes and call it Project Notes.
- Create the basic fields in Project Notes.
- Add a list of related records to the Projects library.

Each of these steps is detailed in the following sections.

 **LET ME TRY IT**

Create a New Bento Library for Notes

1. The first step in creating a related table is to create a new library. Choose File > New Library or click the Add Library (+) button below the Source/Libraries list. Instead of selecting a built-in Bento library, choose the Blank library and name it Project Notes, as shown in Figure 13.4.

> **NOTE**
> There is a built-in Notes library template. Naming this library Project Notes keeps it separate.

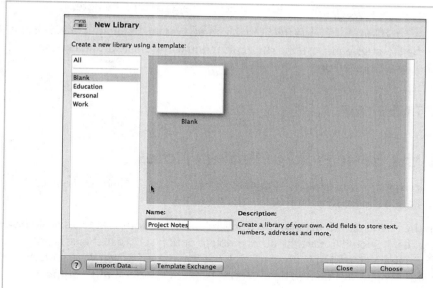

Figure 13.4   *Create a Project Notes library.*

2. The two default fields, Date Created and Date Modified, are in the new
    library as always, although they are not added to the basic table view, as
    shown in Figure 13.5. By default, they are added to the first form view
    (Untitled Form). You can remove them from that view or add them to the
    table view if you want.

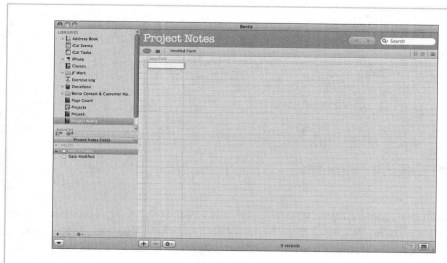

Figure 13.5   *The new library has the two default fields.*

3. In addition to the default fields, you need a field to store the note.

4. It's a good idea to change the library icon to a more meaningful one. Select it in the Libraries pane, use the shortcuts menu (control-click), and choose Choose a Library Icon.

 **LET ME TRY IT**

Create the Basic Field in Project Notes

1. The next step is to create a Notes field. Choose Insert > New Field or click the Add Field (plus) button below the Fields list.

2. In the dialog shown in Figure 13.6, it is relatively obvious that this should be a text field. Should it have the autocomplete option set? That choice is something that you probably need to work out for yourself as you work with the data. If your notes tend to be repetitive (such as "check on this,") autocomplete can be useful; if they are not, autocomplete can be a nuisance.

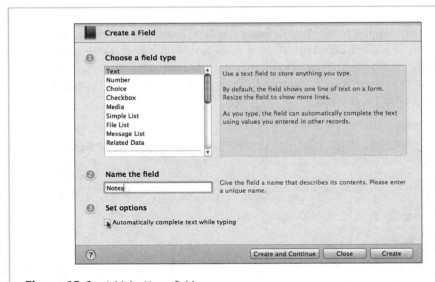

Figure 13.6 *Add the Notes field.*

If you were building a Bento library to use on its own, at this point you would probably start working on one or more forms for your interface. However, in this case, the Project Notes library is going to be used only for related records in the expanded Projects library, so you can move on.

> **NOTE**
> With Bento, you can always come back to make changes. Very few actions in Bento are not reversible (except for the deletion of fields and libraries themselves).

 **LET ME TRY IT**

Add Related Data Fields to the Projects Library

1. You now have a library that can hold related data. All you have to do is add a related data field. The simplest way is to select a form in the Projects library and drag the Project Notes library from the Source/Libraries list onto that form. As you drag it, you see the outline of the related data field. Behind it, you see the form rearranging itself to accommodate the new field. Figure 13.7 shows what it looks like in the middle of the drag-and-drop process before you release the mouse button.

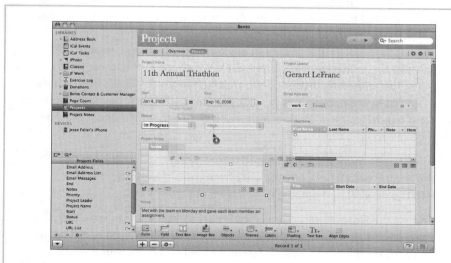

Figure 13.7 *Create a related records list in the Projects library.*

2. When you release the mouse button, the new related data field is created in the form, and the field itself shows up in the Related Data section of the Fields list, as shown in Figure 13.8. If you want to change the name of the related data field from the default name (the name of the related library) to another name, just double-click the name in the Fields list and change it.

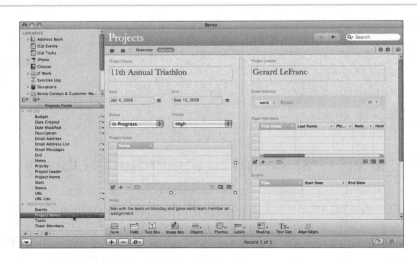

Figure 13.8 *Add the Project Notes library as a related data field.*

3. By default, the fields shown in a related data field are the fields that you have selected to be shown in the related library's table view. If you have not selected any fields for the table view, none show up in the related records list field. In that case or in any other in which you want to add fields to the related records list view, click the icon in the lower right corner of the related records list field, which changes the Fields list to show the fields in the related library. Click the check boxes of the field(s) you want to add to the related records list field into that field and rearrange them as you see fit.

4. To test your changes, add a related record using the + at the lower left of the related data field. Copy the data from the old Notes field and paste it into the new related data field, as shown in Figure 13.9.

5. Choose the Notes library from Libraries list so that you can view the data. At this point, you do need a field in the form, so add a Note Text field. As you can see in Figure 13.10, the pasted note text is visible in the Notes library. You now have a way to enter multiple notes.

6. One further enhancement is to add the Date Modified field for Project Notes to the related records list in Projects, as shown in Figure 13.11.

7. You can sort on this field to find the most recently modified notes and review them as shown in Figure 13.12.

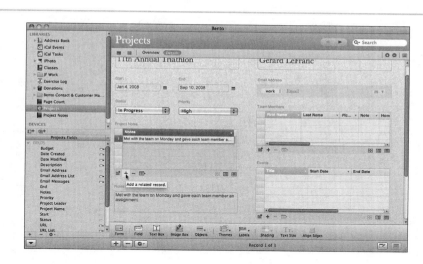

Figure 13.9 *Add a related record.*

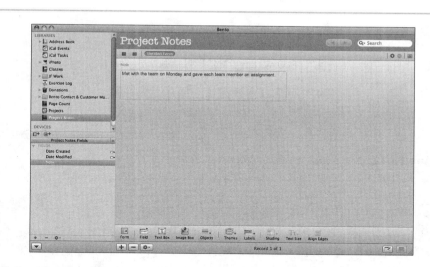

Figure 13.10 *The related Notes records are updated automatically from Projects.*

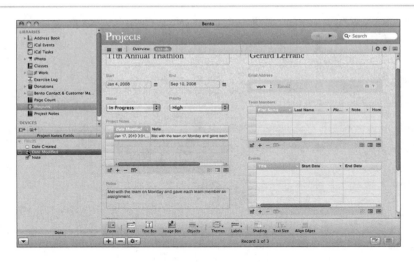

Figure 13.11   *Add Date Modified to the related records list field.*

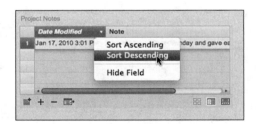

Figure 13.12   *Sort notes the most recent notes are first.*

TIP

You can now remove the old Notes field, but before you do so, consider if you will be updating the library with the iPhone Bento app. Remember that you can modify and display related data in the iPhone Bento app, but you cannot create new related data. By leaving the old Notes field, it will be visible in the iPhone Bento app, and you can always update that field. When you are back at your own computer and have synchronized with iPhone, those comments will be on your Mac, and you can create true related records and delete the temporary data you stored in the old Notes field.

By using related records, you transform the free-format Notes field in the Projects library template into a structured collection of individual notes. In general, any time you can do such a transformation, handling your data is easier.

If you want, you can add more fields to the Notes library, but with Bento, simplicity is key. Maybe you think it would be a good idea to add a Completed field to a note to show that it has been handled. But that duplicates tasks for iCal. If something needs to be completed, it is a task, not a note. Many experienced database designers start to think how new features can be added using the existing data structures that they have. If you need a new feature and need to modify the structure, doing so is easy in Bento. But if you can work a variation on the existing structure, that variation simplifies the structure (and also helps you remember where you have put the data!).

CAUTION

Reusing existing structures does not mean putting multiple types of data in a single field. If you need both a note field and a field to store the phase of a project to which it applies, create a project phase field. When you start cramming unrelated items into single fields, you start to make the database unnecessarily complex. And using special codes or values within a field is a definite no-no. If you are tempted to use a date such as 1/1/2001 to mean "no such data," do not do it. Reusing the structure means getting as much as you can out of the structure you have, but if you need a new field, add it rather than muddying the structure.

 SHOW ME   Media 13.2—A video about creating a related notes table
Access this video file through your registered Web Edition at
my.safaribooksonline.com/9780131388611/media.

Enhancing the Relationship

The Project Notes library that is created here is as generic as can be: You have added only one field to the two default ones. You can use it as related records in almost any library to which notes might apply (which is probably just about any library). Notes can be a record of what you have done, phone calls, or meetings.

In Figure 13.13, you see an additional note added to the Triathlon project.

But wait a minute...the note references a phone call during which you discussed the logo for the triathlon as well as the design of a wine label. It is reasonable that you might discuss two projects when you are talking to one person—particularly as is the case here, when that person is a designer working on both projects.

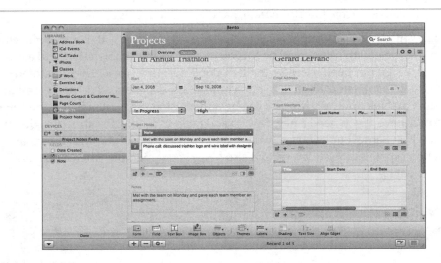

Figure 13.13   *Add more notes using the Projects library.*

You could create two notes, one for each project, but the reality of such a conversation often is that it bounces back and forth from one to another. If you create a single note, as shown in Figure 13.14, it is automatically related to the first project (Triathlon, in this case). You can then go to the other project and add the same note to that project by clicking the icon in the lower left and choosing to add it, as shown in Figure 13.14.

You can use the arrows to the right of the navigation bar to switch between the two projects, and you see that the note is attached to both of them.

But you can do more. You have related the Project Notes library to the Projects library, but the relationship also can work in the other direction. In the Project Notes, drag the Project library icon from the Sources/Libraries list to create a related records list field based on Projects. Figure 13.15 shows the Project Notes library with this related records list added.

An icon in the lower right of a related data field takes you to the selected record in the other library. It opens in the last view (table or form) that you used in browsing that library. In that related record's view, you see a Back button at the right of the navigation bar, as shown in Figure 13.16. The Back button takes you back to the original record. If you have implemented both sides of a relationship as described in this section, you can use the Go to related record button in the lower left of a related records list field and the Back button to switch back and forth from one side of the relationship to the other.

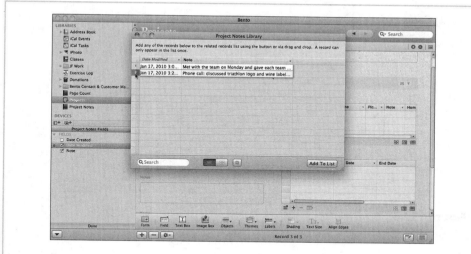

Figure 13.14   *Add a note to more than one project.*

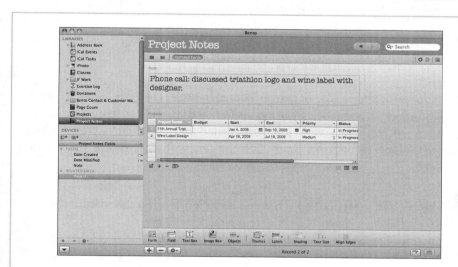

Figure 13.15   *The relationship works in both directions.*

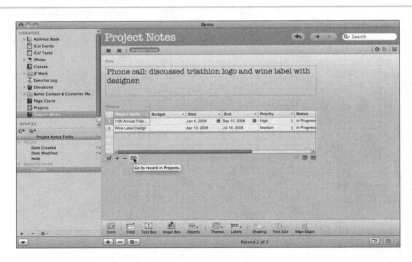

Figure 13.16 *Go to related records.*

 SHOW ME Media 13.3—A video about going to and from related records
Access this video file through your registered Web Edition at
my.safaribooksonline.com/9780131388611/media.

Adding notes (or phone calls or conversations) to project records helps to consoli-date information in one place. By using related records, you can keep them sepa-rate and organized. You can also use Bento's relational capabilities to relate a single record to multiple records in a library, as is the case with a multitopic meeting or phone call.

 SHOW ME Media 13.4—A video about enhancing the relationship
Access this video file through your registered Web Edition at
my.safaribooksonline.com/9780131388611/media.

In addition, you can look at all your Project Notes in table view, sorting them as you want (most likely by date). You can keep track of what you were doing from day to day. As you see each note, you can switch to a form view to look at more details, see the project(s) with which it is associated, and go to the project to get more information.

This ability to switch contexts from what you were doing across all projects to a specific project is a powerful part of Bento's relational functionality. It happens with iCal, which also presents your information in a date-ordered sequence, while at the same time you can organize events and tasks by Bento project or other library.

In general, keeping your Bento libraries relatively simple and focused and using relationships to join them together can make your solutions powerful and robust. Jumbling everything together starts to work against the idea of organizing information. Before you know it, you have reinvented your center desk drawer.

Importing and Exporting Bento Data and Libraries

This chapter shows you how to share your Bento data and libraries by importing and exporting them.

Importing and Exporting Basics

One of the key features of Bento is the ease with which data can be imported and exported. In Chapter 4, "Building a Bento Library from Your Own Data," you saw how to take a data file and import it into Bento, automatically creating a new table from the data. It is a simple process that can quickly bring legacy data, data from the Web, or any other data in a supported format into Bento.

Bento supports input formats including spreadsheets from Excel and Numbers (part of iWork) as well as tab-delimited files such as those from AppleWorks along with comma-separated-value (CSV) files. And, as noted in Chapter 4, if you happen to have data that is in yet another format, you frequently can export it in an intermediate format to a third application and, from there, save it or export it in a supported format.

This chapter expands on Chapter 4 by showing you how to import data into an existing library; it also shows you how to export data from Bento. You also learn to export not just the data, but an entire Bento library including its forms.

Importing Data into an Existing Bento Library

Importing data has a number of variations:

- You may have a Bento table with no data and you want to import data from an external file.

- Your Bento table may have some data already and you want to add data with your import.

- Your Bento table may or may not have some data, and it may have some fields. With your import, you want to add new fields and data for them.

The process described in this section applies to all these variations.

The example used in this section is a familiar task for authors and editors of books: It can be summed up in the question, "How is the page count coming?" In addition to all the other considerations in writing a book, this is something that needs to be managed so that the book comes in on target. Because books are usually written with word-processing software such as Microsoft Word or Pages and because the figures and illustrations are created separately from the text, it is important to find a way to approximate the number of printed pages in each chapter.

For many book layouts, a simple formula is used:

- One word-processing page is approximately one laid-out page in a book. (In fact, many authors and publishers use word styles that have fonts, font size, and margins that make this approximation more accurate. A page typed in Helvetica 42 will not wind up being anywhere close to a laid-out page in a standard book font.)

- One figure with its caption, figure number, and white-space margins above and below is approximately half or a third of a laid-out page.

For a book of several hundred pages, this formula is reasonably accurate, at least for the purposes of tracking page count until the pages are actually laid out. For any individual page, it may be somewhat off. Authors and editors frequently keep track of page count with a spreadsheet, such as the one shown in Figure 14.1. Note that the Total column is a calculation that allocates a third of a page to each figure.

Here is one way to import data from the external data source into a Bento table with no data. (You can compare this to the import procedure described in Chapter 4 where the table was automatically created from the data.)

 **LET ME TRY IT**

Create a New Table for Imported Data

1. Create the new table as shown in Figure 14.2.

2. Add the first three text fields: Title, Pages, and Figures.

3. Add a calculation field for Chapter Pages. Title is a text field; Pages and Figures are number fields. The Chapter Pages field is a calculation field (shown in Figure 14.3).

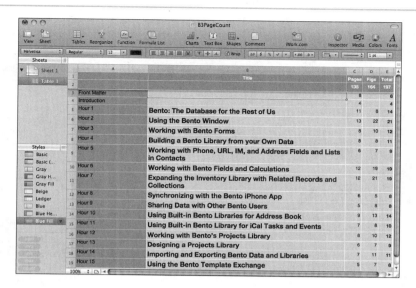

Figure 14.1   *Page count data in a Numbers spreadsheet.*

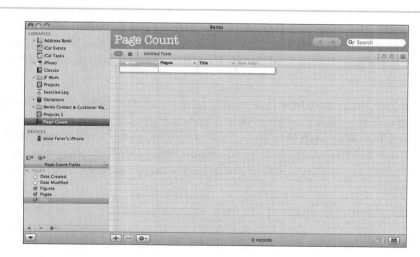

Figure 14.2   *Create the Bento table.*

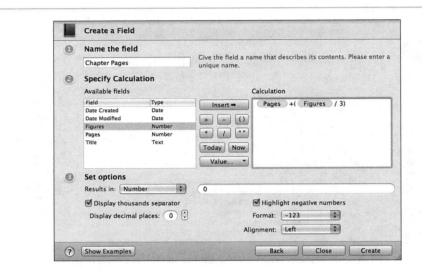

Figure 14.3   *Use a calculation for the Chapter Pages field.*

4. Choose File > Import > File to open the Import dialog, as shown in Figure 14.4. You can select a Numbers or Excel spreadsheet as well as a text file with comma or tab delimiters. This example shows the use of a CSV file because it is very slightly more complicated that importing from a spreadsheet.

5. If Bento senses that the first record of the file contains field names (Bento) or column headings (spreadsheet), it attempts to match them. If there is not an exact match between a column heading in the spreadsheet and a Bento field name, Bento does not import the data by default. However, you can use the pop-up menu to refine the import settings, as shown in Figure 14.5.

> **TIP**
> You can also use the double-headed arrows to rearrange the sequence of the imported fields.

6. As pointed out in Chapter 4, you can adjust the starting record and decide if you want the starting record to be used as titles.

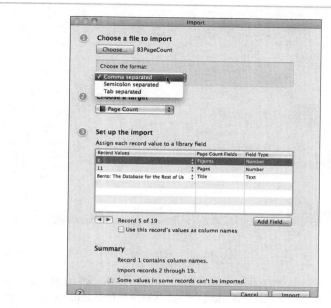

Figure 14.4   *Select import settings.*

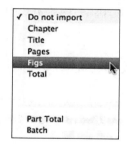

Figure 14.5   *Modify field import settings.*

Figure 14.6 shows the imported data. Note that the appropriate columns are summarized by showing the summary row.

 SHOW ME   Media 14.1—A video about creating a new table for imported data

Access this video file through your registered Web Edition at
my.safaribooksonline.com/9780131388611/media.

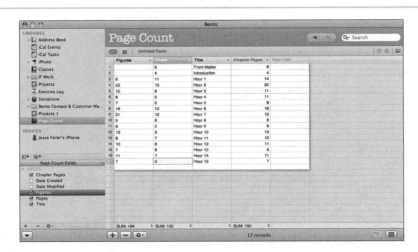

Figure 14.6 *Select import settings.*

You can also copy and paste data into a Bento table view. Select the part of the spreadsheet you want to use and then copy it to the Clipboard as you normally would do. Then, in the Bento table view, click in the cell that you want to be the upper left cell of the imported data—then paste the data. Rows and columns can then be added manually as needed. In most cases, you do not want to add columns in this way, so the upper left cell of your imported data is in the appropriate column (that is, a Pages spreadsheet cell in the Pages column of the blank row of the Bento table view).

 SHOW ME   Media 14.2—A video about importing data by pasting into table view
Access this video file through your registered Web Edition at
my.safaribooksonline.com/9780131388611/media.

 **LET ME TRY IT**

Exporting Bento Data

You often want to go in the other direction — exporting data from Bento to another format. You might do this to share your data with someone who doesn't have Bento, for example.

1. Choose File > Export to export a file from the current library.

   Your export options (Numbers, Excel, Text, and Template) are shown in Figure 14.7.

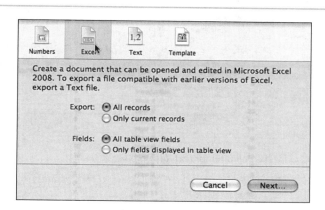

Figure 14.7 *Bento has a number of export options.*

2. Whether you are exporting to Numbers, Excel, or a text file, your first choice is whether to select all records in the Bento library or just the current records (those you have found as the result of a search).

3. In addition, you can choose to export all the library's fields or just those shown in the table view.

4. If you are exporting text data, you can choose the delimiter, as shown in Figure 14.8.

5. Click Next. You will be asked to choose a file name. Click Save and Bento does the rest.

 SHOW ME Media 14.3—A video about exporting Bento data
Access this video file through your registered Web Edition at
my.safaribooksonline.com/9780131388611/media.

NOTE
Related records are not exported from Bento.

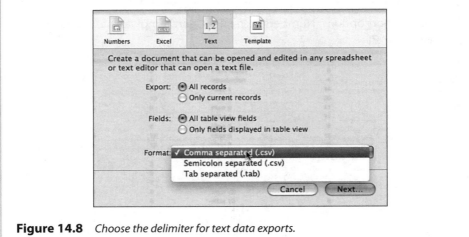

Figure 14.8 *Choose the delimiter for text data exports.*

Importing and Exporting Libraries

You can import and export libraries as templates. This lets you share your both your library structure (including forms and related libraries) with others.

💁 *Templates also make possible the Bento Template Exchange, described in Chapter 15.*

Exporting Bento Libraries as Templates

Exporting a Bento library as a template starts with File > Export. Choose the Template tab at the top to open the dialog, as shown in Figure 14.9.

Unlike exporting to a file, when you export a Bento library template, you can include related tables. When you have selected any related tables, click Next; you are asked to select a name for the file, and that is all you have to do.

Importing Bento Libraries as Templates

Importing is just as easy as exporting. Choose File > Import > Template and then select the template file to import. Click Open, and the library (or libraries) are imported into Bento. You can start to use them right away.

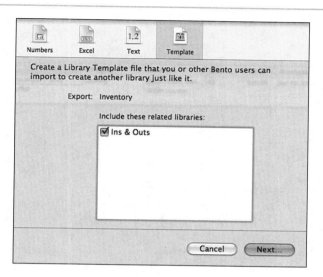

Figure 14.9 *Export a Bento library.*

 TELL ME MORE Media 14.4—A discussion about design considerations for templates

Access this audio recording through your registered Web Edition at my.safaribooksonline.com/9780131388611/media.

Using the Bento Template Exchange

Expand your Bento resources with the Bento Template Exchange.

Exploring the Bento Template Exchange

Bento templates let you share your Bento library designs with other people and use their libraries with your own data. Bento has set up the Bento Template Exchange to facilitate sharing of templates. You can find it at www.filemaker.com/templates; you can also go to it by clicking the Template Exchange button at the lower left area of the New Library window shown in Figure 15.1.

The Bento Template Exchange lets you browse templates by category as well as by popularity. Each template has a small screenshot and a brief description; you can also click to open a larger image. And, of course, you can download a template and actually try it out. This is the best way to get familiar with it.

Figure 15.2 shows a typical landing page for the Bento Template Exchange (the actual templates vary from time to time).

The Bento Template Exchange is a great resource for learning about Bento, in part, because you can see what other people are doing with Bento. As you can see in Figure 15.3, the templates are grouped into categories. This lets you see how people approach very specific problems with Bento.

The Bento Template Exchange is a great way to find libraries that you can use as-is or customize for your own purposes.

When you find one you like (or just want to explore further), click the Download Now button. It will show up in your browser's Downloads window and in your Downloads folder. Just double-click the downloaded template, and it will be imported into Bento. If several libraries are involved, they will all be imported, as you can see in Figure 15.4: Bento Contact & Customer Manager consists of three related libraries.

After you have it in Bento, you can discard the downloaded template file.

Show Me: Exploring the Bento Template Exchange

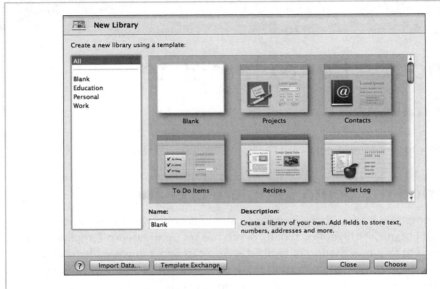

Figure 15.1 *Use the Bento Template Exchange.*

Figure 15.2 *Browse current listings on the Template Exchange.*

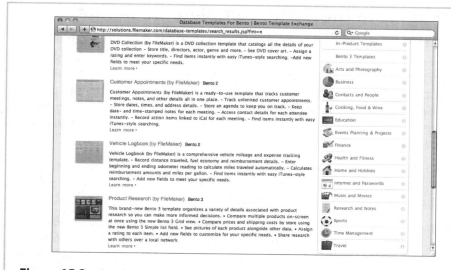

Figure 15.3   *See the categories of Bento templates that are available.*

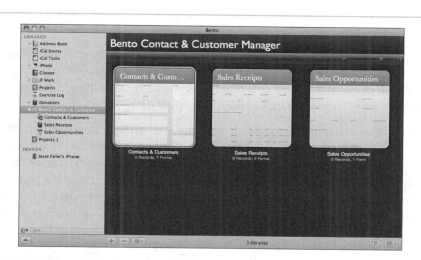

Figure 15.4   *Several related libraries may be installed in the template.*

  SHOW ME   Media 15.1—A video about exploring the Bento
Template Exchange

*Access this video file through your registered Web Edition at
my.safaribooksonline.com/9780131388611/media.*

Learning from the Bento Template Exchange

There are two ways to take advantage of the Bento categories. First, you can make a beeline for a category that interests you or in which you are involved. You may be quite expert in the subject matter, and you will likely find other people who have converted their expertise into Bento templates that may be mysterious to people not used to the general subject area. You may find ideas for how you can better manage your work and data both with a Bento template, but also in the way in which the data is organized and displayed.

You can also explore a category about which you know very little and where you need a helping hand from someone more experienced. In either case, you will most likely find new ideas and techniques from which you can profit.

As you browse the categories, you will find a multitude of templates and ideas for using Bento. You will also notice a number of templates developed by FileMaker, the developer of Bento. These sometimes demonstrate the use of more advanced features in complex solutions to real-life problems.

Often, you will find very specific Bento templates: managing your group's perform-ance gigs, several approaches to keeping sermons fresh, a fairly large number of wine cellar templates, and even templates for tracking Materials Safety Data Sheets and radio advertising.

With Bento, it's easy to get right down to business (or play), so you probably do not want to spend a great deal of time doing homework. But if you are in the right mood, you can spend a good deal of time browsing through the templates and learning how other people look at Bento and their data.

One of the most common mistakes people make when they start thinking about databases for their work is to think that their problems are unique—either unique to their own operations or unique to their particular lines of work. One of the les-sons to be learned from the Bento Template Exchange is that there is a great deal in common among all of the people who are building Bento templates: They all want to organize their data, and it turns out that their data seems to be remarkably similar no matter what businesses they are in.

Think about how people must be using Bento and these templates so that you can get a better idea of how to structure your own libraries. As you think about these templates and Bento, you may realize that some of the things you are used to doing are not easy to do in Bento. That is not a limitation of Bento in most cases: It is an example of procedures that you may be following now that are not needed when you use Bento.

Perhaps the most common example is assigning a number to each item you are tracking, whether it is a club date for your band, an order for a product, or a project that you and other people will work on together. Many people have evolved complex numbering structures for these cases. For example, your first order for 2011 might be 2011-1. And if it is for a green awning, the number might be 2011-1-GA.

This is a very bad type of number for two reasons:

- If the order changes, the number changes. If it turns out the customer wants a blue awning rather than a green one, you either change the number from 2011-1-GA to 2011-1-BA or leave the number as it was for the green awning and make a note that it will be fulfilled by shipping a blue awning.

- This type of numbering makes it difficult to handle orders with multiple different items (and also complicates many other issues).

Database designers know that the best identification numbers are meaningless so that you can change the characteristics of the items being dealt with. Bento makes this simple because the internal ID numbers for your records are totally internal to Bento. You can use Counter field types to generate unique serial numbers, but you do not have to do that. This is an example of Bento "just working." One of the keys to working successfully with Bento is not to think about the database: Think about your business, and Bento will take care of the data.

Another common error is collecting information in a database because it is available. You can easily wind up entering everything from wind speed to temperature and rainfall amounts for each day's data that you collect. However, unless your business is related to the weather, there is not much reason to do so. Furthermore, that data is easily obtainable on the Internet, even for past dates. If you need that information just in case it might be important, it is often the best solution to collect the data you care about (sales figures, for example) and then if there is an anomaly that you want to investigate, go back to easily available data to see what if anything was different about the days in question. Collecting and entering the data for each day is often a waste of time.

Sharing Your Templates

The Bento Template Exchange relies on volunteers sharing their templates and ideas. When you create a template, the data is removed from the template, so you do not have to worry about revealing your finances or your customer list.

Sharing your templates is a good way of sharing your expertise with others (both Bento and business-specific expertise); it also is a good way of improving your Bento libraries. When you start to share a template, click Submit Template at the right of the basic Bento Template Exchange page shown previously in Figure 15.2 (located at www.filemaker.com/templates). This starts the submission process, as shown in Figure 15.5.

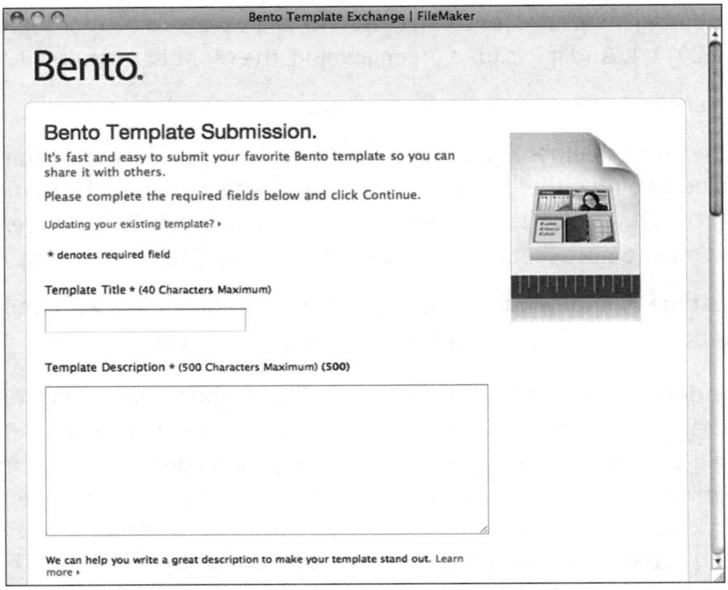

Figure 15.5 *Begin to submit your template.*

The people at Bento understand that you know your template better than anyone else, so they have given you a questionnaire that helps to organize the information about your template. You may think your template is one-of-a-kind and that nothing else anywhere in the world (much less in the Bento Template Exchange) even comes close, but the people at Bento know that your template is going to be interesting and useful to people if it is positioned in the world of other templates so that it can be found and compared.

You will need to provide a title and select a category for your template, and you also need to indicate if it is designed for Bento 2 or Bento 3. (Bento 1 did not support templates.) All Bento 2 templates should be usable in Bento 3, but there are some features in Bento 3 that are not supported in Bento 2.

There are three basic questions to answer when you submit your template:

- What is it? Some templates are clearly identifiable, such as an attendance tracker for a class or a calorie counter. Others represent a synthesis of several tasks that may only be recognizable to people in your particular line of work. In such cases, you do not have a ready-to-use term to describe your template, so you may fall back on a more generic term such as Retail Florist Order Organizer or Theater Prop and Costume Tracker. The generic terms "organizer," "tracker," and "manager" are paired with very specific terms that help people understand your template's capabilities.

- What does it do? This lets you describe your template in a bit more detail.

- How does it do it? Here is where you can hone in on your template's functionality. Your Retail Florist Order Organizer may keep track of customers and their orders, but it might also keep track of a wish list for each customer or particular likes and dislikes ("no white carnations," for example). This would be a good place to let people know if you are relying on other data sources such as Address Book or iCal; it also is a good place to point out if your Bento library supports synchronization or sharing. These specific features help people to choose among similar templates.

All of this needs to be provided in no more than 500 words. If you cannot describe your template in this space, maybe your template is very specific to the way you work and would not easily be used by someone else. More likely, you can think about it a little more and find a way to describe it succinctly so that as many people as possible can use it.

Whether you use Bento and its built-in templates just as they are when you first launch Bento or whether you create your own templates or download new ones from the Bento Template Exchange, Bento provides you with the tools you need to take control of your data without becoming a database manager. Your job is managing your business, your life, and your adventures. Bento's task is to help you do that without getting in the way.

index

A

accounts, 13-14

adding
   calculation fields to Exercise Log, 87-89
   data to related data fields, 116-117
   images to forms with image boxes, 185-186
   records to collections, 123-124
   related data fields, 114
      and its data, 117
      to Projects library, 203-204, 207
   related records, 187-191

Address Book, 78, 155
   related records, 187
      adding, 189
   sharing contacts with MobileMe, 193-194
   synchronizing
      with Address Book library, 160-161
      with iPhone, 164-166
      with MobileMe, 161-163
      with PDAs, 167
   updating with Mac OS X data detectors, 168

Address Book library, 155-158
   extending with new fields and forms, 158-160

synchronizing with Address Book, 160-161

Advanced Find, 39-41

Apple, 179
   MobileMe, 12

automatic counter fields, creating and formatting, 103-104

automatic counters, 20

B

basic data import, performing, 67-69

Bento, 1, 7
   accounts, 13-14
   data, 10-11
      exporting, 218-219
      mobility of, 12
   fields, editing, 104-105
   getting started with, 14-16
   overview, 7-9
   programming, 12
   roles of, 11
   tasks, 176

Bento Address Book library, 77

Bento iCal libraries, 176-178

Bento iPhone or iPad app, 1, 131
   creating new libraries, 136-137

Home button, 133-134
   searching libraries, 134

Bento iPhone app library, 137

Bento libraries
   creating for Notes, 200-202
   exporting as templates, 220
   importing as templates, 220
   synchronizing, 195-198

Bento library, templates, 78

Bento Template Exchange, 223
   learning from, 226-227
   sharing, 227-229

Bento windows, 25, 28
   libraries, creating, 28
   records area, 29-30
      Bento window, 25
      creating new, 33-34
      deleting records, 42
      finding data, 38-39
      grid views, 30-31
      printing records, 36-37
      split views, 31-33
      table views, 30
      text data, 35
   table views
      fields, editing, 44
      pasting data into, 43
      records area, 30
      sorting, 42

C

Calculation dialog, 96-97

calculation fields, adding to Exercise Log, 87-89

calculations, 96
  Calculation dialog, 96-97
  Calories Burned field, 100-101
  creating, 98-100
  Duration field, 98

calendars, 174
  multiple calendars, 180

Calories Burned field, 100-101

checkbox fields, 20
  creating and formatting, 102

choice fields, 20
  creating and formatting, 101

choosing themes, 54-55

cleaning up imported data, 74-75

collections, 22-24, 122-123. *See also* Smart Collections
  adding records to, 123-124
  creating
    empty, 123
    from selected records, 124
  Smart collections, 125-127

comma-separated value (CSV), 65

contact data, Contacts library, 85

Contacts library, 77-80
  adding fields and lists, 84-85
  contact data, 85
  fields, 81
    entering contact data, 81-82
  menus, 82-83

copying forms within libraries, 60

counters, automatic counters, 20

CSV (comma-separated value), 65

currency fields, 19
  creating and formatting, 103

customizing
  fields, Projects library, 192-193
  forms
    fields, 56-60
    with themes, 53-55

D

data, 10-11
  basic data import, performing, 67-69
  calendars, managing, 180-181
  cleaning up imported data, 74-75
  contact data, Contacts library, 85
  entering in Contacts library, 81-82
  exporting, 218-219
  finding in records area, 38-39
    Advanced Find, 39-41

importing
  into existing libraries, 213-214
  into new Bento libraries, 69-73
  legacy data, reviewing, 64
  mobility, 12
  organizing, 63-64
  pasting into table views, 43
  securing, 149-150
    database passwords, 151-152
    encrypted fields, 150-151
    locked fields, 152-154
  securing on iPhones or iPad, 144
  synchronizing with MobileMe, 167-168
  tables, creating for imported data, 214-218

data detectors (Mac OS X)
  Mail, iCal, 178-179
  updating Address Book, 168

data elements, 10

data formats, 64-67

data structure, iCal, 175-176

data structuring, 16

database passwords, 151-152

databases, connecting to shared databases, 148

date, fields, 19

date and time field controls, 92-94

deleting
    fields, 91-92
    records, 42
        *from Ins & Outs
        library, 119*
Details form, related
    records from iCal and
    Address Book, 187
Details layout, Projects
    library, 184
duplicating
    fields, 91-92
    forms, 52
Duration field,
    calculations, 98
duration fields, 19

E

editing
    events, iCal, 174
    fields, 104-105
        with table views, 44
empty collections,
    creating, 23
encrypted fields, 20,
    150-151
Energy Saver control
    panel, 196
entering contact data in
    Contacts library, 81-82
events
    iCal, 174
        synchronizing, 182
    naming, 190-191
    sharing with MobileMe,
        193-194
Exercise Log
    calculation fields,
        adding, 87-89

calculations, 96
    *Calculation dialog,
    96-97*
    creating, 98-100
    Duration field, 98
    Calories Burned field,
        100-101
    date and time field
        controls, 92-94
    number fields, 95-96
    start date field, creat-
        ing, 91-92
    stop date field,
        creating, 89-91
existing structures,
    reusing, 207
Export command, 65
exporting
    Bento libraries as
        templates, 220
    data, 218-219

F

fields, 17-21
    Address Book library,
        158-160
    and lists, Contacts
        library, 84-85
    automatic counter
        fields, creating and
        formatting, 103-104
    calculation fields, 87-89
    Calories Burned field,
        100-101
    checkbox fields, 20
        *creating and
        formatting, 102*
    choice fields, 20
        *creating and
        formatting, 101*

Contacts library, 81
    *entering contact
    data, 81-82*
currency fields,
    creating and
    formatting, 103
date and time field
    controls, 92-94
deleting, 91-92
duplicating, 91-92
duration fields, 19
editing, 104-105
    with table views, 44
encrypted fields, 20,
    150-151
file list fields, 20
forms, customizing,
    56-60
locked fields, 152-154
media fields, 19
message list fields, 20
Notes field,
    creating, 202
number fields, creating
    and formatting, 95-96
Projects library, cus-
    tomizing, 192-193
Quantity field, 108
rating fields, 20
    *creating and
    formatting, 104*
related data fields, 20
    adding, 114
    *adding data to,
    116-117*
    formatting, 115
    summarizing, 118
renaming, 91-92
simple lists, 20
start date field,
    creating, 91-92
stop date field,
    creating, 89-91

Fields dialog, 19

Fields pane
Bento window, 25
forms, 51

file list fields, 20

FileMaker Pro, 197

FileMaker Server, 197

finding data, records area, 38-39
Advanced Find, 39-41

form view, 51

formats, data, 64-67

formatting
automatic counter fields, 103-104
calculations, 96
Calculation dialog, 96-97
Duration field, 98
checkbox fields, 102
choice fields, 101
currency fields, 103
number fields, 95-96
rating fields, 104
related data fields, 115

forms, 49
adding images with image boxes, 185-186
Address Book library, 158-160
copying within libraries, 60
customizing with themes, 53-54
choosing themes, 54-55
duplicating, 52
fields, customizing, 56-60
Fields pane, 51
form view, 51

grid view, switching to, 49
relationships, improving, 119-121
renaming, 52
revising with Projects library, 192-193

G

grid views, 30-31
switching to, 49

H

Home button, Bento iPhone app, 133-134
horizontal separators, 57

I-J-K

iCal, 155, 171
data detectors (Mail), 178-179
data structure, 175-176
events, 174
synchronizing, 182
managing calendar data, 180-181
Projects library, 199
related records, 187-188
relationships, 211
Search Results pane, 172
searching, 172-174
To Dos, 171, 174-176

iCal Events, 155

iCal libraries, 176-178

iCal Tasks, 155

identification numbers, 227

image boxes, 185
adding images to forms, 185-186
Projects library, 185

images, adding to forms with image boxes, 185-186

Import Data button, 28

imported data, cleaning up, 74-75

importing
Bento libraries as templates, 220
data
into existing libraries, 213-214
into new Bento libraries, 69-73

improving relationships and forms, 119-121

Ins & Outs library
creating, 109-111
records, deleting, 119
related records, reviewing, 118-119

inventory, tracking with relationships, 112-114

Inventory library, 107-109
Ins & Outs library, creating, 109-111
related records, reviewing, 118-119
tracking inventory with relationships, 112-114

iPad, 131-133

iPhones
Bento iPhone app, 131
creating new libraries, 136-137

Home button,
133-134
*searching
libraries, 134*
securing Bento
data, 144
synchronizing, 129
*with Address Book,
164-166*
with iTunes, 165
synchronizing
libraries with your
computer, 138
*doing your first sync,
140-144*
*same wi-fi network,
138-139*
iPhoto Bento library, 155
iPhoto library, 169-170
iTunes, setting up
iPhone synchronization
with, 165
iWork applications, Pages
and Numbers, 65

L

LAN, shared libraries, 197
legacy data, reviewing, 64
libraries, 12, 22
Address Book library,
155-158
*extending with new
fields and forms,
158-160*
Bento iPhone app, 137
Contacts library, 77-80
*adding fields and
lists, 84-85*
contact data, 85
fields, 81-82
menus, 82-83

copying forms
within, 60
creating, 9, 28
*with Bento iPhone
app, 136-137*
creating for Notes,
200-202
creating new, 25
exporting as
templates, 220
iCal libraries, 176-178
importing as tem-
plates, 220
importing data,
213-214
importing data into
new, 69-73
Ins & Outs library, cre-
ating, 109-111
Inventory library,
107-109
*Ins & Outs library, cre-
ating, 109-111*
*related records,
reviewing, 118-119*
*tracking inventory
with relationships,
112-114*
iPhoto library, 169-170
Notes library, 28
Project Notes
library, 202
Projects library, 183-
185, 198-199
Details layout, 184
*enhancing relation-
ships, 207-211*
*fields and forms, cus-
tomizing, 192-193*
image boxes, 185
Notes, 199-200
*related data fields,
adding,
203-204, 207*
templates, 184

searching with Bento
iPhone or iPad app,
134
shared libraries, 147
connecting to, 148
synchronizing
between iPhone or
iPad and your
computer, 138-144
Libraries & Fields pane, 44
library folders, 45-46
library icons, 46-47
Libraries pane, Bento
window, 25
library folders, Libraries &
Fields pane, 45-46
library icons, Libraries &
Fields pane, 46-47
lists, and fields (Contacts
library), 84-85
Lock/Unlock Encrypted
Fields command, 151
locked fields, 152-154
Login Options, 13

M

Mac, templates, 137
Mac OS X, TextEdit, 66
Mac OS X data detectors,
updating Address
Book, 168
MacBook, synchronizing,
195-196
Mail
data detectors, iCal,
178-179
related records, 191
managing calendar data,
180-181

media fields, 19, 107

menus, Contacts library, 82-83

message list fields, 20

MobileMe, 12, 130
  Address Book contacts, creating and sharing, 193-194
  calendar events, creating and sharing, 193-194
  iCal, synchronizing, 182
  synchronizing
    with Address Book, 161-163
    data, 167-168
    with iPhone, 166

N

naming
  events, 190-191
  tasks, 190-191
  templates, 226

navigation bar, records area, 29

New Library dialog, 25, 79

Newton, 179

Notes, 199-200
  creating Notes field, 202
  creating new Bento library for, 200-202

Notes field, creating, 202

Notes library, 28

number fields, creating and formatting (Exercise Log), 95-96

numbers, fields, 19

O

organizing data, 63-64

P

Pages and Numbers files, 65

passwords
  database passwords, 151-152
  sharing passwords, 154

pasting data into table views, 43

PDAs, synchronizing with Address Book, 167

PDF (Portable Document Format), 65-66

PDF button, 37

performing syncs, 144

Portable Document Format (PDF), 65-66

preferences, setting, 47-48

printing records, 36-37

procedural programming, 12

programming, 12

project management, 199

Project Notes library, 202

Projects library, 183-185, 198-199
  Details layout, 184
  fields and forms, customizing, 192-193
  image boxes, 185
  Notes, 199-200
  related data fields, adding, 203-204, 207

relationships, enhancing, 207-211
  templates, 184

Q

Quantity field, 108

R

rating fields, 20
  creating and formatting, 104

records, 21-22
  adding to collections, 123-124
  collections, creating, 124
  deleting, 42
    from Ins & Outs library, 119
  printing, 36-37
  related records
    adding, 187-191
    Mail, 191

records area, 29-30
  Advanced Find, 39-41

records area
  Bento window, 25
  creating new, 33-34
  deleting records, 42
  finding data, 38-39
  grid views, 30-31
  printing records, 36-37
  split views, 31-33
  table views, 30
  text data, 35
    spell checking, 35-36

related data fields, 20
  adding, 114
    data to, 116-117
    to Projects library,
      203-204, 207
  adding with data, 117
  formatting, 115
  summarizing, 118
related records
  adding, 187-191
  Mail, 191
  reviewing, 118-119
relationships
  creating by dragging
    libraries onto forms,
    112-114
  improving, 119-121
  Projects library,
    207-211
  related data fields, 117
  tracking inventory,
    112-114
renaming
  fields, 91-92
  forms, 52
reusing existing struc-
  tures, 207
reviewing
  legacy data, 64
  related records,
    118-119
revising forms, Projects
  library, 192-193
Rich Text Format (RTF), 65
roles of Bento, 11
RTF (Rich Text Format), 65

S

"same wi-fi network,"
  138-139
Search Results pane,
  iCal, 172
searching
  iCal, 172-174
  libraries, Bento iPhone
    or iPad app, 134
securing
  Bento data on your
    iPhone or iPad, 144
  data, 149-150
    database passwords,
      151-152
    encrypted fields,
      150-151
    locked fields, 152-154
security, 149-150
  database passwords,
    151-152
  encrypted fields,
    150-151
  locked fields, 152-154
Set Bento preferences,
  47-48
shared databases, con-
  necting to, 148
shared libraries, 147
  connecting to, 148
  LAN, 197
  synchronizing, 197-198
sharing, 145
  setting up, 145-147
  templates, 227-229
  versus synchronization,
    129-130

sharing passwords, 154
simple lists, 20
Smart Collections, 22-24,
  125-127, 158
Smart Groups, 157-158
sorting table views, 42
spacers, 57
spell checking, text data,
  35-36
split views, 31-33
spreadsheets, 75
start date field, creating in
  Exercise Log, 91-92
stop date field, creating in
  Exercise Log, 89-91
summarizing related data
  fields, 118
switching
  between Bento and
    Address Book, 155
  to grid view, 49
synchronizing, 195
  Address Book
    with iPhone, 164-166
    with MobileMe,
      161-163
    with PDAs, 167
  Address Book and
    Address Book library,
    160-161
  Bento libraries, 195-198
  data with MobileMe,
    167-168
  iCal events, 182
  libraries between
    iPhone or iPad and
    your computer,
    138-144
  versus sharing, 129-130

syncs, performing, 144

System Preferences,
   managing accounts, 13

T

table views, 42
   fields, editing, 44
   pasting data into, 43
   records area, 30
   sorting, 42

tables, creating for
   imported data, 214-218

tasks, 176
   naming, 190-191

templates, 26
   Bento library, 78
   Bento Template
      Exchange, 223
      *learning from,
         226-227*
      sharing, 227-229
   exporting Bento
      libraries as, 220
   importing Bento
      libraries as, 220
   Mac, 137
   naming, 226
   Projects library, 184

text, fields, 19

text data, 35
   spell checking, 35-36

TextEdit, 66

themes, forms, 53-54
   choosing themes,
      54-55

time, fields, 19

To Dos, iCal, 171, 174-176

tracking inventory with
   relationships, 112-114

U

updating Address Book
   with Mac OS X data
   detectors, 168

V

views
   form view, 51
   grid views, 30
   split views, 31-33
   table views, 30
      fields, editing, 44
      pasting data into, 43
      records area, 30
      sorting, 42

W-X-Y-Z

windows, Bento windows,
   25, 28
   libraries, creating, 28
   records area, 29-30
      Bento window, 25
      creating new, 33-34
      deleting records, 42
      finding data, 38-39
      grid views, 30-31
      *printing records,
         36-37*
      split views, 31-33
      table views, 30
      text data, 35
   table views
      fields, editing, 44
      pasting data into, 43
      records area, 30
      sorting, 42